PAPERCRAFT PR

for Special Occasions

PAPERCRAFT PROJECTS
for Special Occasions

SÌNE CHESTERMAN

GUILD OF MASTER CRAFTSMAN PUBLICATIONS

Dedication

To my parents
for their early encouragement in the arts and sciences.

First published 2002 by
Guild of Master Craftsman Publications Ltd
166 High Street, Lewes,
East Sussex, BN7 1XN

ISBN 1 86108 253 3

A catalogue record of this book is available from the British Library.

Cover and finished photography by Anthony Bailey, Guild of Master Craftsmen
Photographic Studio

Cover and book design by Chris Halls at Mind's Eye Design, Lewes

Typeface: Goudy and Frenchscript

Colour origination by Viscan Graphics (Singapore)

Printed and bound by Kyodo Printing (Singapore) under the supervision of
MRM Graphics, Winslow, Buckinghamshire, UK

Contents

Introduction   1

GETTING STARTED
Materials and Equipment   4
Papercraft Techniques   6

PROJECTS

Introduction

If you think back to your own childhood, you will remember the joy of holding coloured pens in your hands or stirring brightly coloured powder paints and making your first marks on paper. Or maybe you have young children of your own and have marvelled at the pleasure they experienced when experimenting with paper for the first time – tasting, tearing, scrunching it into balls – and creating lots of mess! The aim of this book is to rekindle those first creative urges – either to create pieces to please yourself or to use as ways of developing your children's practical and creative skills and to build their confidence.

So, there's no excuse. Why not pull out from drawers and cupboards those long-hoarded pieces of paper that you have been meaning to use up. Paper is an excellent medium – adaptable, easy to work with, available in lots of colours and textures – with little outlay for tools and materials. All the projects in this book have been made from readily available paper and card. It is fun to discover new materials: specialist papers are very attractive, sometimes embedded with flowers or seeds. But really, there is no need to go to great lengths to source special materials – just keep it simple. This is especially advisable if you are making projects with children. You should expect to use a lot of paper, card, glue and paint, and you don't want to worry about spending too much money on these basics. And, once the inevitable happens and your creative spirit and confidence takes over – you will be looking at all kinds of new ways to make use of paper and card to create appealing gifts for friends and family.

This brings me to a second reason why I think it is a good idea to have an accessible book on papercraft. How often do you hear of a friend's birthday, or have a special celebration coming up and you want to give someone a personal gift? Or your children want to make something unique for a birthday or Christmas present? My approach to papercraft is that it should be a fun and individual way to celebrate a special event and to let someone know you are thinking about them.

In this book, I have tried to consider a range of ages, ability and the amount of time you have to work on something. Some of the projects are simple (but effective), while others reflect the longer time spent on them and require greater precision. Much use has been made of items such as craft and trimming knives, but these can easily be replaced by safety scissors if you are working with children. With the supervision of an adult, most of the projects are child-friendly.

As you will see from the Contents list at the beginning of this book, the projects are grouped by special and seasonal festive occasions throughout the year, and each is represented by a greetings card or selection of cards, a gift box, a room display and dining table decoration. Many of the projects can be adapted and extended to suit alternative occasions. And, as you work through the book and gain confidence, you should treat them as stepping stones for developing your own creative ideas.

Have lots of fun!

Getting Started

Materials and Equipment

MATERIALS

Paper and card

I have used only basic, easily available paper and card such as that sold in dedicated stationery shops or departments of larger stores and art and craft shops. For economy, you may find a local printing firm has some stock left over from a print run, though you'll probably have to buy a minimum quantity. It is also worth looking in the business section of your telephone directory – 'Paper and Board' or 'Paper Merchants' is probably a good start. These sources may supply free sample books and large sheets, or sell cheaply packs of various colours and weights of a particular range of paper.

Special papers

I regularly use foil-backed card which always impresses friends and relatives on a special occasion – particularly for gift boxes and tags. A roll of plain or coloured corrugated card is also very useful. It can be adapted to any number of projects and can be painted different colours if you wish.

Accessories

Ribbon in a range of colours, lengths and thicknesses finishes off a gift nicely (see, for example, the celebration gift box, page 142). Do seek out accessories – sometimes found objects like beads or shells or even pieces of string can enhance the decoration of a papercraft project.

A small selection of basic materials to get you started.

Recycled materials

It is always worth hanging on to cardboard containers and packaging for comestibles and other household items to recycle into containers such as vases and boxes. These might include: salt or breadcrumb containers, toilet paper tubes, cereal packages and other flat cardboard packaging. The latter is particularly helpful for making reusable stencils. I have a large store of salvaged packaging items that can be usefully adapted to all kinds of applications.

EQUIPMENT

You only need a few basic pieces of equipment and, as with paper and card, these are readily available from craft stores or suppliers if you do not own them already.

Drawing equipment
Pencils (2B and HB)
Pencil sharpener
Eraser
Metal-edged ruler, 305mm (12in)
Long ruler, 450mm (18in)

Cutting equipment
A craft knife (scalpel, or with snap-off blades)
Heavy duty trimming knife with straight blades (for cutting thicker card)
Pair of sharp scissors with pointed blades that cut the full length of the blade
Embroidery scissors (for finer work)
Children's safety scissors. I find curves are easier to cut with scissors and safety or school scissors are generally curved at the ends.

A3 double-sided self-heal cutting mat. Though initially costly, this is really a worthwhile investment when cutting with knives – the blades last longer and the working surface remains even and undamaged.

Adhesives
Stick and multipurpose adhesives
PVA glue
Spray adhesives (for large areas)
Small glue spreaders (commercially available, or, alternatively, make your own from round or flat toothpicks)
Roll of clear adhesive tape
Cotton-buds, or swabs (for cleaning off any excess glue)

Useful equipment
Old, blunt scissors (for cutting foil)
Tweezers (for getting into small spaces)
Needle-nose pliers (to hold items securely in place while they dry)
Clothes pegs (to use as above)
Narrow drinking straws (useful for making the Chinese lanterns, page 147)
Coloured pencils
Coloured felt-tip pens
Watercolour paints
Apron
Cleaning products and cloths (for the inevitable messy moments!)

Optional equipment
A compass and protractor are helpful for copying the templates for some projects, but only if you prefer to draw your own instead of photocopying the ones that I have provided in this book.

Papercraft Techniques

Before you begin work on a papercraft project, it is worth spending some time familiarizing yourself with a few simple techniques that appear again and again in different forms in this book. As well as this, I've included one or two tips to help you.

Paper grain

Some papers have grain and others do not. Machine-made papers and cards have a grain, whereas handmade papers do not. This is because they are individually made, often from recycled materials. Folding 'against the grain' – especially when using thicker or heavier paper and card – can produce unsightly rough edges. In this book, I have used only paper and thin card to avoid problems with grain. Where I have used thicker card, it has been kept purposely flat.

Test the direction of the grain by bending (without creasing) a sheet of paper in half several times to gauge the spring. Then turn the sheet 90° clockwise and bend again to feel the difference in tension. Whichever bends more easily will be 'with the grain', i.e. along the line of the fibres.

Another technique is to take a spare piece of your chosen paper and tear a strip down the length of the paper. If it tears neatly, with a smooth edge, you have found the direction of the grain; if it is hard to control the tear, it is likely to be against the grain.

Transferring patterns

If your pattern is already full scale, it is much easier to transfer your design to your chosen paper or card. To do this, you can either photocopy or trace the pattern using tracing paper and a pencil.

If your pattern needs enlarging, you can either use a photocopier to get the correct size, making sure you have the right percentage, or alternatively, use the traditional squaring up method. This entails tracing your original and then drawing a 1cm (⅜in) grid over it. Taking a fresh piece of tracing paper – first making sure it will be large enough to contain the enlargement – and, using a ruler and pencil, draw a grid to match your needs. For example, for a 200% enlargement, draw out a 2cm (¾in) grid. Once you have drawn your grid, you can copy over the pattern centimetre square by square, following your original.

Origami

Although we often use paper to write letters or other information, it has been adapted by many cultures to perform different functions, both practical and decorative, for thousands of years. Today's paper folding techniques or 'mechanics' – including the techniques I have used in this book – are based on a very ancient art originated by the Japanese called origami. Quite simply, the word is comprised of 'ori' which means to fold and 'kami' which means paper. Origami transforms flat paper into

This miniature paper reproduction of the Webb Theatre, dated 1850, features a scene from a production of Red Riding Hood. It is a beautiful example of the way in which papercraft techniques have evolved and combined into many diverse and exciting forms over the years.

objects that can move or become three-dimensional – from paper airplanes to pop-up characters and toy theatres (see above). It is really a form of engineering.

The language of papercraft

For the projects in this book, I make use of the basic terminology for instructing simple folding techniques so that you are familiar with the language of papercraft. The main technique you will come across is called 'mountain and valley' folding. As it sounds, 'mountain' folds are those that form peaks in the paper, and 'valley' folds are those which form V shapes in the paper. Used together in

a pattern, they produce a concertina effect. The following symbols represent the kind of fold – mountain or valley – or cut signified on the templates for each project to guide you.

Mountain fold

— · — · — · — · — · — · — · — · — · — · —

Valley fold

- -

Cutting line

————————————————————————

Fold already made

————————————————————————

Creasing

When you are ready to make a crease in the paper, crease firmly and carefully. Creases should also be accurate. Incorrect creases lead to folds that are out of alignment with one another. Make sure you have a flat surface to work on, and fold the paper so the crease is facing you rather than away from you.

Folding and scoring

When using card, it is helpful to score a line so that it folds precisely where you want it and without forming 'wrinkles'.

Before you commit to scoring something, do practise on a scrap test sheet first. If any broken folded edges result, you know you will need to score the folds first on your actual piece.

There are a number of tools you can use to score paper. Darning needles work well. These are available with either blunt or semi-sharp tips; both can be used for different folding effects. For most folding, I recommend using a semi-sharp needle mounted into a cork or piece of dowel to help create sharp, precise score lines, but try to avoid cutting too deeply as this will create a weakness in the paper. It needs to be able to bend, but without breaking. To create rounded, folded corners, use a blunt darning needle to score the curved line.

To create a flexible crease on an item that needs to be used again and again – a box lid on a gift box, for example – you need to cut-score. The technique of cut-scoring involves making a series of cuts in the form of dashes, rather than a line.

A useful item for creating folds is a ruler. For a precise fold, place the ruler very close to the line and fold against it.

Scoring can be done on either side of your item – the right or the wrong side – as long as you are careful. Whichever side you choose to score, try to avoid using a pencil mark to get a straight line for scoring. Sometimes this is necessary, but I find the resultant marks difficult to erase and they are a little unsightly on the surface of a finished project. Instead, try the following. Make a pinprick at either end of your desired fold line; this provides two points between which you can then form a straight line. Do remember to always score along the fold lines before cutting out your paper template.

Why not practise each of the methods described above and see which works best for you with your chosen material.

Cutting

Like scoring, there is more than one way to cut paper! I have at least three different cutting implements for this purpose: knives, scalpels and a range of scissors.

For perfect straight lines, it is best to use a sharp knife, running it along the line against a metal-edged ruler.

To create curves in your card or paper, a sharp pair of scissors is easier to use (or a pair of safety scissors when working with small children). If you wish to use a knife, though, hold it in the hand like a pen.

For sharply rounded corners, first trim around the outline – about 3mm (⅛in) from the edge – leaving only a narrow strip of excess paper to push against the scissors.

When using foil-backed card, you achieve a better cut if you cut with the right or good side facing upwards.

Curving

To curve rounded sections, I find it easiest to pull the paper against the edge of a table, gently repeating this curving motion until it achieves the desired effect. Alternatively, roll the paper around a cylindrical object.

To glue curves into position, just apply a few dabs of glue to the interior so that excess glue won't be visible on the exterior of the project.

Colouring edges

On some projects, for example those using foil-backed card, colouring in the cut edge of the card enhances the finished presentation. When colouring in cut edges with pencil, use the flat side rather than the tip of the pencil; this gives a much softer, more subtle effect. I find that light grey is often effective for matching any pale colours, and dark grey for darker colours – but you might prefer to use a coloured pencil or pen to match brighter colours.

If you are using watercolour paints, try to ensure the colour stays within the edges of your pattern and doesn't spill over the edge, although if working on a project with children, this is much less necessary. The point here is to suggest a coloured edge rather than be precise.

Using a cylindrical object is an effective way to create a curve in your paper project.

Using selective colour on the edges adds an authentic touch to paper flower projects.

Using adhesives

Which adhesive you use to glue your projects can be key to its overall effect. If, for example, you use PVA glue on paper which is too thin to withstand it, it will probably wrinkle, thereby destroying your effect. For larger items, you will need a glue that is strong and dries quickly. Spray adhesive is often used by professionals in art and design for its strength and flexibility. If you make a mistake, you can often quickly peel the paper apart again until you get it in the correct position. It is widely available from art and craft shops. Its one disadvantage is that its smell can be quite pervasive and unpleasant, so do work with it in an area with good ventilation.

Finishing

If you are making a gift box or other item which you intend to last some time, I recommend applying a coat of clear acrylic varnish. This will help to seal the card from moisture and dirt while it is on display. Do be careful which varnish you select, though – some turn yellow with age, or may be too 'heavy' for the card you are using. Sometimes, the varnish can deepen the colour of the surface of the card or paint you are using, which can be quite effective, but it is probably best to experiment with one or two brands on test pieces of paper, first, to gauge the effects.

Templates

Most of the projects are accompanied by templates. Sometimes they are reproduced to full size, but are often half or a quarter of the original size to fit the format of this book. Where this occurs, enlarge the template on a photocopier, adapting the percentage as

desired, or use the squaring up method (see page 6). Be careful to check the dimensions for minor discrepancies before beginning a project.

I have included metric measurements with the nearest equivalent imperial conversions for the dimensions of each project. Again, with any enlargement or reduction in the size of the project, you will need to adjust these by the correct proportions to fit.

The templates feature all the correct dimensions, but you can enlarge or reduce as desired.

Getting started

While you want to achieve good work, with papercraft, the emphasis is on having fun. And, understandably, your work environment is not always ideal. Often it is the case that you only have the edge of a kitchen table to lay out your materials and work. If you have a dedicated workspace – or something similar – all the better, but really, make the best of whatever space you have; don't let it hamper your enthusiasm for the papercraft itself.

Wherever you work, the important thing is to try to work on a clean, stable, level surface.

Once you have a space to begin work, check the list of materials and equipment you require. For some projects, you can substitute items with alternatives. Read all the instructions through before attempting the first step in the method; this will help to avoid mistakes later.

With all the techniques required for the projects in this book, always keep in mind accuracy. When working with children, this is less crucial – and there is nothing worse than dampening a child's enthusiasm for creativity by drawing their attention to mistakes in folding or gluing. But when making projects yourself, do try to be as precise as possible when drawing out and using the templates. Be focused when cutting out to ensure that you are following the right lines. Fold carefully and precisely for crisp folds. Keeping these things in mind will help you achieve your desired results much more efficiently.

Metric and imperial conversions

The measurements in this book are given in metric and expressed as millimetres as appropriate. Imperial conversions are given in brackets. Do not mix the two systems; always use one in preference to the other to avoid mistakes.

METRIC CONVERSION TABLE
inches to millimetres

inches	mm	inches	mm	inches	mm
⅛	3	9	229	30	762
¼	6	10	254	31	787
⅜	10	11	279	32	813
½	13	12	305	33	838
⅝	16	13	330	34	864
¾	19	14	356	35	889
⅞	22	15	381	36	914
1	25	16	406	37	940
1¼	32	17	432	38	965
1½	38	18	457	39	991
1¾	44	19	483	40	1016
2	51	20	508	41	1041
2½	64	21	533	42	1067
3	76	22	559	43	1092
3½	89	23	584	44	1118
4	102	24	610	45	1143
4½	114	25	635	46	1168
5	127	26	660	47	1194
6	152	27	686	48	1219

Projects

Birthday

Floral stencil greetings cards

Octahedron gift box

Pied Piper spiral mobile

Sunflowers centrepiece

Floral stencil greetings cards

These attractive cards make use of simple stencils based on wild flowers: marsh marigold, common mallow, lesser periwinkle, sweet violet and wood sorrel. They are certain to delight a friend or relative on their birthday.

MATERIALS AND EQUIPMENT

Single sheet of A4 paper (per birthday card)
Thick card, 146 x 210mm (5¾ x 8¼in) (if making a template for a larger card)
Coloured pencils, pens and/or paints
Drawing pencil
Craft and trimming knives

METHOD

STEP 1 First transfer the templates provided (see Figs 1.1a to 1.1e, pages 18–19) onto your selected paper. You can do this by tracing or photocopying the floral motif. To trace, use a pencil and mark the motif onto the lower right-hand quarter of the sheet of A4 paper. Next, fold the paper twice – once in half across the paper, then turn 90° and fold in half a second time along the length of the paper. Alternatively, copy the floral motif onto a piece of thick card and cut out the design to make a reusable stencil to create outlines or areas to fill in with coloured pencils, pens or paints.

STEP 2 An alternative option to transferring the designs is to create your own. If you have a computer with the appropriate software, you can scan in your favourite motifs or create your own originals and print them off on a colour printer directly onto the A4 sheet of paper. Computer art can be very effective and allows you to produce copies of the same image time after time.

All actual size

Fig 1.1a

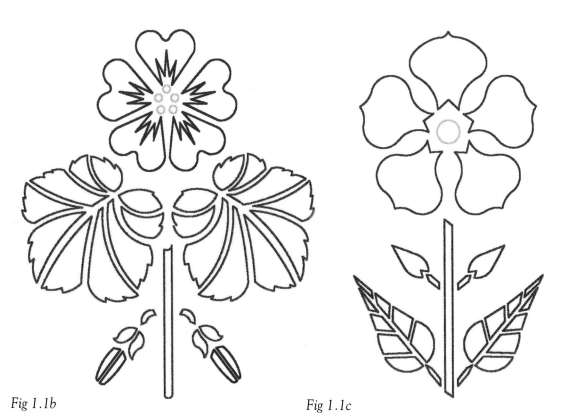

Fig 1.1b

Fig 1.1c

Fig 1.1d

Fig 1.1e

Octahedron gift box

This floral gift box is formed from one sheet of card and folded into eight equilateral triangles to form an octahedron. It is the perfect foil for small gifts – items of jewellery like a ring or necklace, a 5ml bottle of perfume or some favourite sweets. For larger gifts, simply enlarge the dimensions on the template.

MATERIALS AND EQUIPMENT

A4 sheet of medium thickness card
Multipurpose adhesive
Drawing pencil
Scoring tool
Trimming knife
Coloured pencils, pens or paint
Metal-edged ruler

METHOD

STEP 1 Transfer the floral motifs onto the piece of card. The floral motifs are the same as those that appear on the birthday card, but reproduced at a quarter of the size. Follow the pattern and the measurements detailed on the template provided (see Fig 1.2, overleaf).

STEP 2 Score along the fold lines, following the dash marks, and then cut out along the outside edge of the box.

STEP 3 Crease along all the fold lines to shape the box.

STEP 4 Apply multipurpose glue to the centre section of the base tab – the base is the one blank face of the octahedron – leaving a tiny 10mm (⅜in) gap at each end to insert the gift tag afterwards. Next, glue the remaining two tabs and, once the gift is inserted, close the top tabs.

STEP 5 For the accompanying gift tag, first draw the shape (or design it on the computer) and transfer the reduced floral motif.

STEP 6 Cut out the tag, then write your personal greetings message on the reverse.

STEP 7 Fold the tabs and slip the tag into the glue-free slots at either end of the base tab.

Enlarge 132%

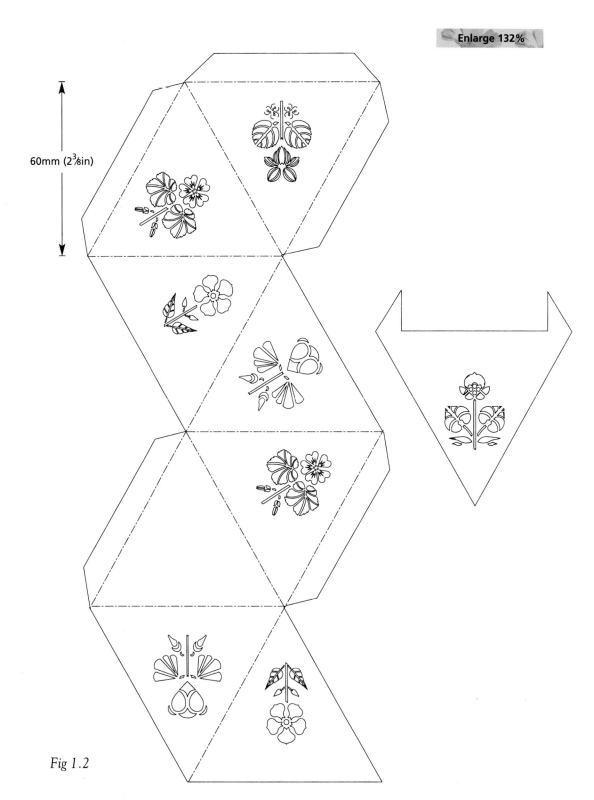

60mm (2³⁄₈in)

Fig 1.2

Pied Piper spiral mobile

The story of the *Pied Piper of Hamelin* is recreated here in the form of a mobile –
the rats follow the Pied Piper down to the river, while the children spiral up the
mountain, lured by his magical tune.

The mobile is very flexible. It can be suspended as a room decoration – perhaps
for a children's party, or alternatively, it could be given as a present;
it will collapse easily for flat packing.

23

MATERIALS AND EQUIPMENT

Thick white card (380 micron), 203 x 241mm (8 x 9½in)
Watercolour paints (or alternative medium)
Paintbrushes
Nylon thread
Pencil
Trimming knife

METHOD

STEP 1 Transfer the spiral template provided (see Fig 1.3, facing opposite) to your card, enlarging it to the size you require. This will be far quicker than drawing it by hand.

STEP 2 Draw the characters along the spiral: the Pied Piper at either end and facing in opposite directions, with the rats and children facing each of the pipers. Execute the drawings in whatever style you feel most comfortable: realistic and detailed, abstract or in silhouette. Do ensure all the characters are separate, though, so that they rest on the top line of the grass and will fold without distorting the card.

STEP 3 Paint the front of the characters, then the grass and then the river.

STEP 4 Carefully cut out the spiral and around the individual characters.

STEP 5 Turn over the card and paint the reverse side.

STEP 6 Returning to the original side, gently fold the base of each character to stand upright once the spiral mobile is mounted.

STEP 7 To suspend the mobile, add a length of nylon thread through the top of the Pied Piper's hat.

STEP 8 Finally, in keeping with the original story, in which the Pier Piper turns away from the river, fold the path near to the bottom end of the mobile.

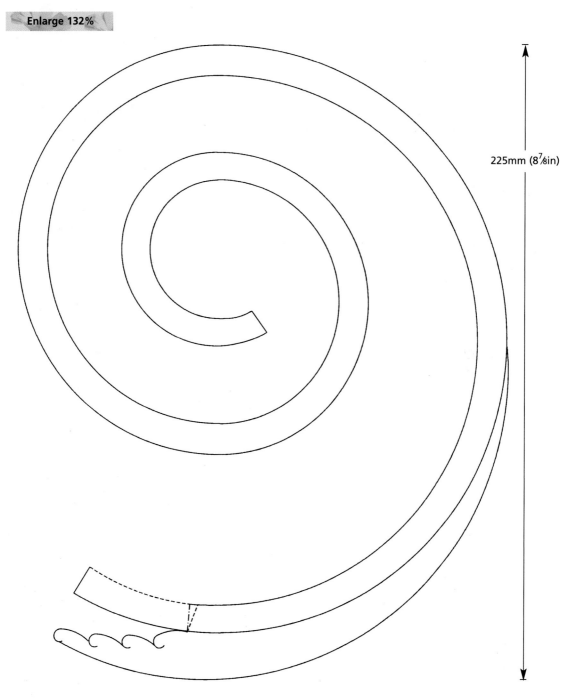

Enlarge 132%

225mm (8⅞in)

Fig 1.3

Sunflowers centrepiece

This centrepiece is really two projects in one – a very jolly bouquet of paper sunflowers and the striking vase in which to display them. Each part involves different folding techniques.

RED VASE

MATERIALS AND EQUIPMENT

Sheet of card, 520 x 639mm (20½ x 25⅛in)
Cardboard tube container, 65mm (2⁹⁄₁₆in) in diameter, 152mm (6in) in length
Drawing pencil
Scoring tool
Metal-edged ruler
Trimming knife

METHOD

STEP 1 Mark, score and cut out the vase using the template (see Fig 1.4, overleaf), including the small slit – which is slightly wider than the width of length R.

STEP 2 Crease the fold lines on the lengths that form a decorative waistband around the middle of the vase, marked L for left and R for right, following the marks for the valley and mountain folds on the template. Open the creases except for the two long mountain folds on either side of each length.

STEP 3 Crease along the lines at either end of the cylinder, marked A and B, starting with the longest fold. Fold those on the right at B first, then turn the card over and crease the lines at A.

STEP 4 Turn the card over once more. Crease along the line down the centre of the whole piece and fold over A from left to right to form a central fold.

STEP 5 Form a cylinder by curving the cardboard, rolling it gently into shape. Pass lengths L and R between the two layers of card and through the slit, pulling the card gently together to form a cylindrical shape, with one side just slipping inside the other.

STEP 6 Slide the cardboard container into the cylinder. This helps to keep the vase stable while you finish constructing it and provides permanent solidity once complete to hold the paper flowers. Gently pull lengths L and R to tighten the cylinder, then separate them, and crease them flat so they wrap around the cylinder and join at the front.

STEP 7 Next, make the folds on each of the lengths. With the vase base nearest you, take length L and, starting with the inner crease, fold the first two valley creases, then the three mountain creases. The end of the length will form a 45° angle.

STEP 8 With length R, fold as a concertina. Where the two lengths will conjoin, fold R over L so the two open triangular ends interlock. Finally, slip the loose end of R under L to secure (see main photo for the finished appearance).

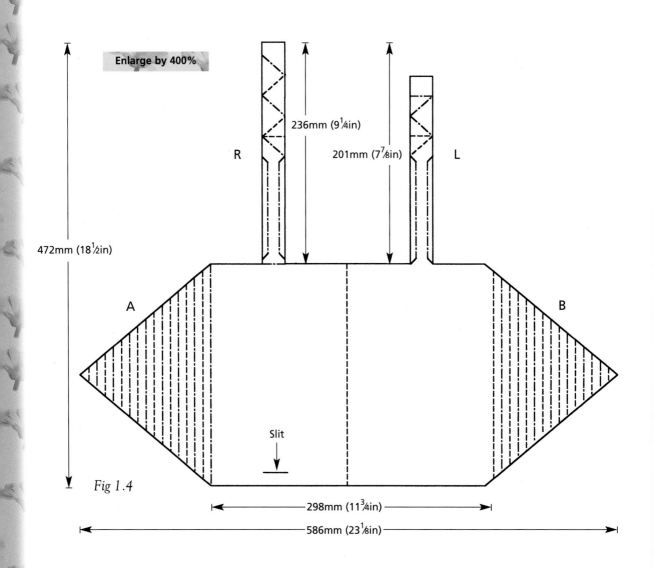

Fig 1.4

FIRST SUNFLOWER

There are two variations of this design.

MATERIALS AND EQUIPMENT

Two strips of card, one red, one orange, 295 x 16mm (11⅝ x ⅝in)
Two strips of card, one red, one orange, 572 x 16mm (22½ x ⅝in)
A4 sheet of yellow card
A4 sheet of green card
Pencil
Metal-edged ruler
Trimming knife
Multipurpose adhesive
Five small rubber bands
Wood dowel (or wooden spoon), minimum 229 x 10mm (9 x ⅜in) in diameter

METHOD

STEP 1 Start by making the concertina-shaped seed heads with the orange and red card. Glue the end of one strip onto the end of the other, at right angles, as precisely as possible. Fold the strips back and forth over each other to form a concertina length. Once complete, glue the loose flap at the end and trim.

STEP 2 Curl the concertina length to form a circle and glue the ends together. Use a clothes peg to secure it while it dries.

STEP 3 Make a second seed head section with the remaining strips of orange and red card. Once the glue is dry, ease out the larger circle and fit it over the first to form the seed head.

STEP 4 Transfer and then cut out the stalk (see Fig 1.5a) and sepal sections (see Fig 1.5b) from the green card (see overleaf).

STEP 5 Place the seed head onto the remaining green card, draw a circle around it and cut out the circle keeping within the line so that it is slightly smaller.

STEP 6 Add a dab of glue onto the base of the seed head and fit onto the circle you have made.

STEP 7 Gently curve the stalk section against the piece of dowel and then glue it with an overlap of 13mm (½in), using the rubber bands to hold it in place while drying.

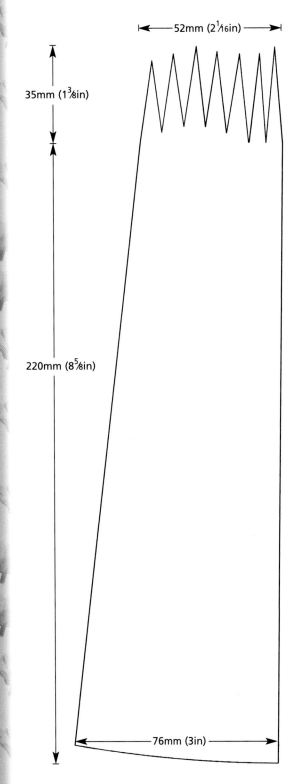

|← 52mm (2¹⁄₁₆in) →|

35mm (1⅜in)

220mm (8⅝in)

76mm (3in)

Fig 1.5a

STEP 8 Transfer the petals template (see Fig 1.5c, opposite) onto yellow card and cut out.

STEP 9 Apply glue to the edge of the concertina seed head and wrap the petal strip around it.

STEP 10 Glue the 18 triangular sections on the strip, onto the base of the seed head.

STEP 11 While this dries, fit the green sepal section over the end of the stalk. Enlarge the hole to an oval for the stalk to fit at an angle. Glue the stalk and sepals to the head.

Fig 1.5b

Enlarge all by 132%

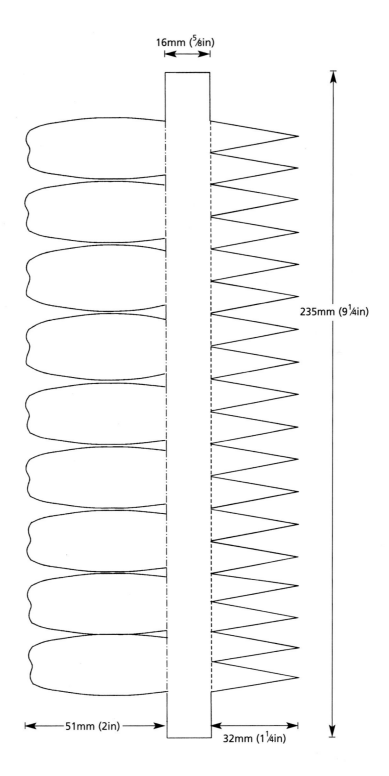

16mm ($\frac{5}{8}$in)

235mm (9$\frac{1}{4}$in)

51mm (2in)

32mm (1$\frac{1}{4}$in)

Fig 1.5c

SECOND SUNFLOWER

MATERIALS AND EQUIPMENT

Sheet of yellow card, 216mm (8½in) square
Two strips of card, one red, one orange, each 295 x 16mm (11⅝in x ⅝in)
Sheet of green card, 421 x 102mm (16⅝ x 4in)
Clothes peg
Pencil
Metal-edged ruler
Trimming knife
Pair of safety scissors (optional)
Multipurpose adhesive
Eight small rubber bands
Wood dowel, minimum 305 x 10mm (12 x ⅜in) in diameter
(alternatively, a wooden spoon)

METHOD

STEP 1 Start the second sunflower by making a seed head from the red and orange strips of card. See instructions for the first sunflower, steps 1 and 2.

STEP 2 Transfer the template for the circle of flowers (see Fig 1.6a, facing opposite) onto the sheet of yellow card and cut out.

STEP 3 Starting at A and going clockwise, spread a curved line of glue to form a semicircle between the base of the petals and the triangular sections. Curve round the left (unglued) half of the flower, over the right half and press together to form two layers of petals.

STEP 4 Working from the back of the flower, spread glue on the inside of the triangles and onto the orange and red concertina shapes you have made. Insert the concertina into the flower head and secure in place with the glued triangles.

STEP 5 Make the stem as for the first sunflower, step 7, but extending the length to approximately 305mm (12in).

Enlarge both by 132%

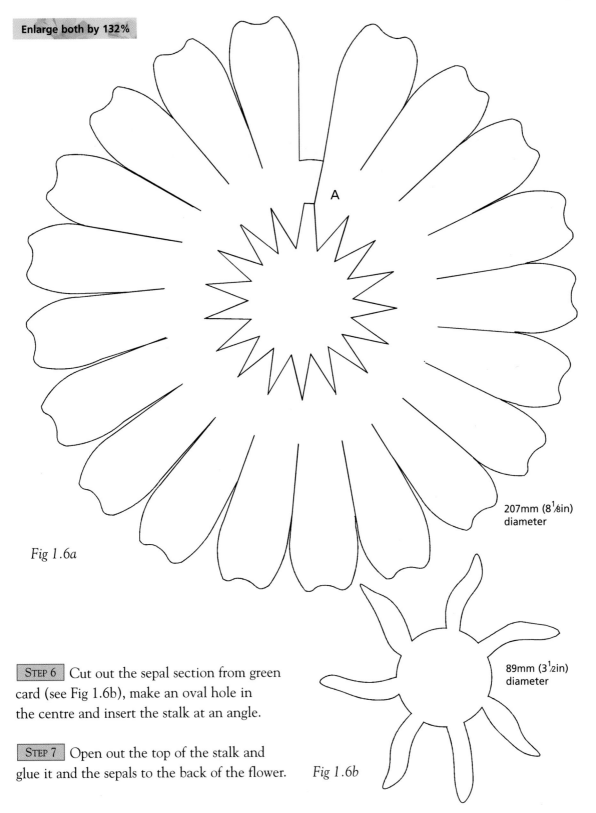

A

Fig 1.6a

207mm (8$\frac{1}{8}$in)
diameter

89mm (3$\frac{1}{2}$in)
diameter

STEP 6   Cut out the sepal section from green
card (see Fig 1.6b), make an oval hole in
the centre and insert the stalk at an angle.

STEP 7   Open out the top of the stalk and
glue it and the sepals to the back of the flower.   *Fig 1.6b*

Valentine's Day

Valentine's Day card

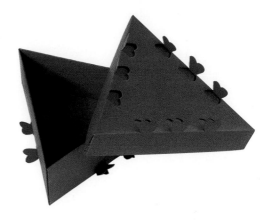

Triangular gift box

Double hearts display

Birds and flower centrepiece

Valentine's Day card

By historical accident, St Valentine has long been associated with sending tokens of affection to special loved ones. Using a combination of paper folding and cutting techniques, this design is a contemporary twist on the traditional card.

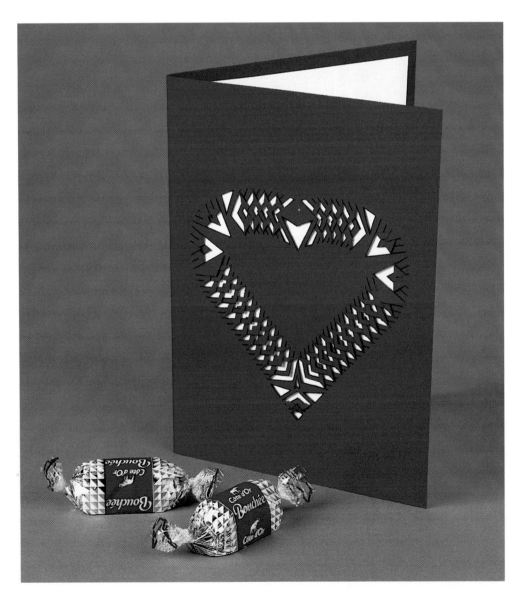

MATERIALS AND EQUIPMENT

Single A4 sheet of red card
Single sheet of A4 paper (any matching pale colour)
Stick adhesive
Craft knife
Metal-edged ruler

METHOD

STEP 1 Transfer the pattern to your card (see Fig 2.1, overleaf) so that the design features in the centre of the right-hand side of the card.

STEP 2 Checking the photograph as you work, carefully cut out and remove the nine cut-out sections, and then the V-shaped lines to create vents.

STEP 3 Keeping the card flat, rotate the card through 90°.

STEP 4 Begin folding the V sections, starting with the second V from the top centre of the heart, folding alternate V shapes and tucking each section under the previous-but-one, gradually working towards yourself while folding these V sections upwards.

STEP 5 Form the two shapes at the corner of the design by folding the largest V section in half, then lifting the card from the surface and easing the point through the smallest V. Crease flat.

STEP 6 Rotate the card 180° and work on the reverse end of the heart shape as before.

STEP 7 Turn the card to work down one side at a time, finishing at the base of the heart shape by tucking the largest V into the smallest.

STEP 8 Fold the card in half so that it will stand up.

STEP 9 Mount the lighter coloured paper to the centre of the card, neatly creasing it down the middle and secure it in place with a little stick adhesive.

Actual size

Fig 2.1

Triangular gift box

This pretty Valentine's gift box is an ideal way to present a gift to a loved one.
It can be amply filled with a selection of chocolates or other small, desirable items
to celebrate the day.

MATERIALS AND EQUIPMENT

A2 sheet of red card
Scoring tool
Metal-edged ruler
Trimming knife
Multipurpose adhesive

METHOD

STEP 1 To make the gift box the same size as my original, enlarge the template on the photocopier to make sure the measurements are accurate. Transfer the patterns for the lid and base of the gift box onto the red card (see Figs 2.2a and b, facing opposite).

STEP 2 Start by carefully cutting around the heart shapes.

STEP 3 Score all fold lines on both the base and lid.

STEP 4 Carefully cut out the lid and the base and then crease all the folds.

STEP 5 Construct the lid. Spread glue on the three short tabs shown, and on a 19mm (¾in) strip around the edge of the central triangular top of the lid, on the side which will form the inside of the lid, avoiding the nine heart sections.

STEP 6 In one movement, fold in the three sides, tucking in the corner tabs and sticking the sides to the lid top. Ensure there is no excess glue on the heart shapes.

STEP 7 Once dry, manipulate the heart shapes so that they stand erect from the surface of the lid.

STEP 8 Turn to the base. First ensure that, once folded inwards, the hearts on the base will pass through the V-shaped slits on the edge of the base. Cuts are required on the fold line, on either side of each V shape so that each slit measures 17mm (¹¹⁄₁₆in) across.

STEP 9 Apply glue to the small corner tabs and to a 25mm (1in) strip around the inside of the triangular base. Fold the base into shape, passing the hearts through the slits and tucking in the corner tabs, pressing to secure.

STEP 10 You can glue the hearts around the edge of the base to the sides or leave them unfolded as shown.

STEP 11 Make a little gift tag of your own design or copy the one I have made (as shown on the previous page) to place inside the box.

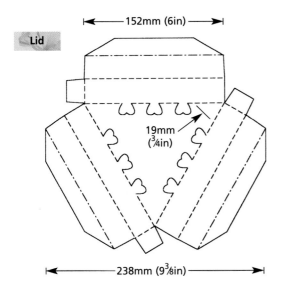

Lid

← 152mm (6in) →

19mm
(³⁄₄in)

← 238mm (9³⁄₈in) →

Fig 2.2a

Enlarge by 400%

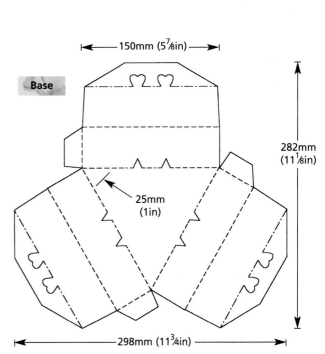

Base

← 150mm (5⁷⁄₈in) →

25mm
(1in)

282mm
(11¹⁄₈in)

Fig 2.2b   ← 298mm (11³⁄₄in) →

Double hearts display

This unusual design makes a striking, romantic display on Valentine's Day.
If you like, dress it with shiny red ribbon for added sparkle.

MATERIALS AND EQUIPMENT

Two sheets of A4 card, one red, one silver
Stick adhesive
Craft knife
Pair of safety scissors (optional)
Length of nylon thread (optional)

METHOD

STEP 1 Transfer the pattern by photocopying
or copying by hand onto your pieces of card
(see Figs 2.3a and 2.3b, overleaf). Cut out the
shapes with a craft knife or, if working with
young children, a pair of safety scissors. The
two heart shapes (see Fig 2.3b) are designed to
be cut apart in one flowing curve to emphasise
their unity.

STEP 2 Crease the two tabs, insert them
through the cut slits marked on the first
template and glue into place.

STEP 3 To create a three-dimensional effect
with the two red hearts, open them outwards
and gently lean them against one another so
that they meet in the middle.

STEP 4 If you wish to display the double
hearts from the ceiling or mounted at the
window, attach a length of nylon thread
discreetly to the top of the display.

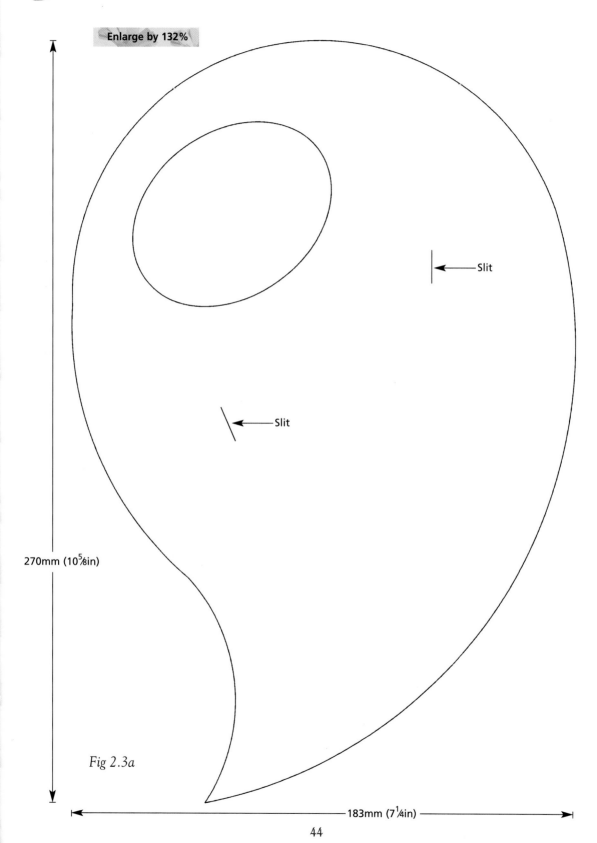

Enlarge by 132%

← Slit

← Slit

270mm (10⅝in)

Fig 2.3a

183mm (7¼in)

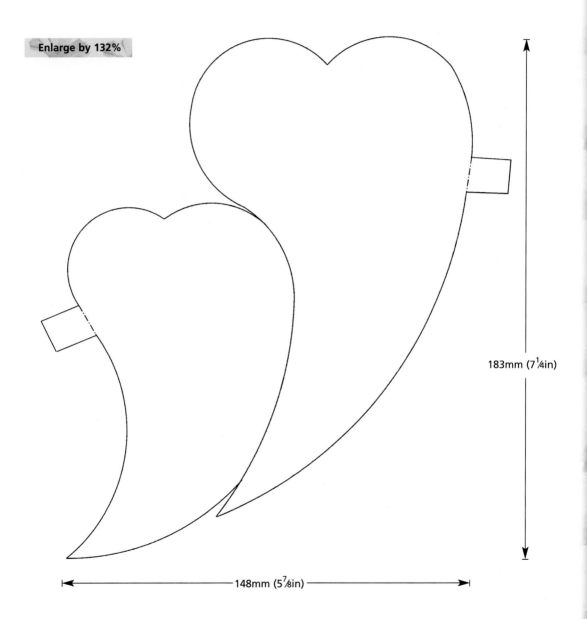

Enlarge by 132%

183mm (7¼in)

148mm (5⅞in)

Fig 2.3b

Birds and flower centrepiece

This charming design for a centrepiece evolved from making paper lovebirds into
a more complex scene, with two birds resting on a birdbath
and a pretty, windblown flower.

BIRDBATH

MATERIALS AND EQUIPMENT

Single paper plate, 229mm (9in) in diameter
Watercolour paints (various colours)
Paintbrush
Jar filled with water (to dilute the paint)
Metal-edged ruler

METHOD

STEP 1 Take one of your paper plates and fold it in half, ready to paint. Decide how you would like to work your design: either copying the one shown or creating your own.

STEP 2 Decorate with the watercolour paints. On my original, I have painted a brick backdrop with a rippling water-filled bath inside a blue stone bowl.

PENTAGONAL FLOWER

MATERIALS AND EQUIPMENT

Foil-backed card, 114mm (4½in) square
Two narrow strips of foil, 203 x 2mm (8 x ⁵⁄₆₄in) (insert from a packet of coffee)
Multipurpose adhesive
Trimming knife
Pair of old scissors (for cutting foil)
Metal-edged ruler
Scoring tool

METHOD

STEP 1 Transfer the pentagonal design on the template (see Fig 2.4, below) to the paper side of the foil-backed card. Score along the fold lines marked on the template. These should fold easily, starting with the five longest mountain creases.

STEP 2 Fold the two foil strips in half and curl them. Do this by dragging your thumbnail down each length – or use a pair of scissors to do the same action. Once curled into lengths, glue them to the centre of the flower and the flower itself to the edge of the water feature (see main photo, page 46).

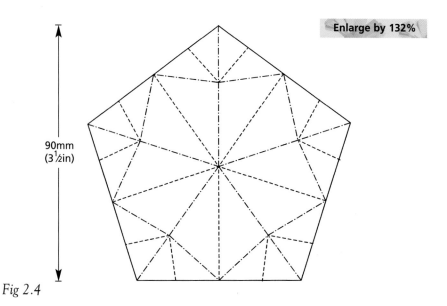

90mm
(3½in)

Enlarge by 132%

Fig 2.4

WHITE BIRD

MATERIALS AND EQUIPMENT

A4 sheet of white paper
Scissors
Pencil
Stick and multipurpose adhesive

METHOD

STEP 1 Transfer the pattern to the white paper (see Fig 2.5) twice.

STEP 2 Cut around the outer edge of the pattern, leaving a margin of about 3mm (⅛in) to make the job a little easier. Next, cut out the outline itself and along the lines shown to create the individual sections radiating from the body.

STEP 3 Curl the long tail feathers and the crest by wrapping them around a pencil.

STEP 4 Next, glue the front – or beak – sections on top of one another to shape the bird's head.

STEP 5 First curve – then glue together – the wing sections third along from the bird's head

STEP 6 Glue the bird to the edge of the plate.

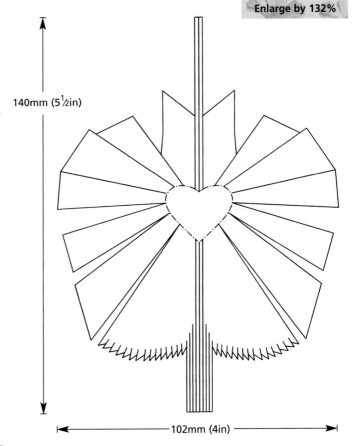

Enlarge by 132%

140mm (5½in)

102mm (4in)

Fig 2.5

Mother's Day

Mother's Day card

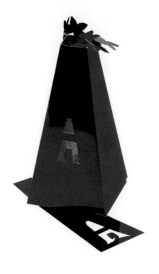

Pyramid gift box

Christmas cactus display

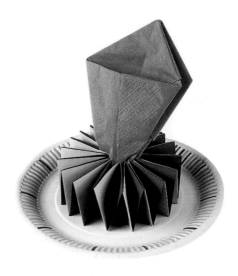

Poke napkin centrepiece

Mother's Day card

Our pretty Mother's Day card matches perfectly the feel of early spring with its peach and pink floral theme. It makes use of three-dimensional paper folding and cutting techniques to transform the greetings card into a display.

MATERIALS AND EQUIPMENT

Single A4 sheet of paper (desired colour)
Pencil
Metal-edged ruler
Craft knife

METHOD

STEP 1 Transfer the template to your paper, first enlarging it on the photocopier to get the original size (see Fig 3.1, overleaf).

STEP 2 Draw or key on the computer your Mother's Day design and greetings onto the front of the card as shown on the template, leaving a gap at the upper and lower edges to feature the decorative flap. For the original, I took a section of one of my photos, rotated it clockwise by 90°, resized, copied and pasted it into position in the lower left-hand rectangle of an A4 sheet of paper (see Fig 3.1). Add your text before printing.

STEP 3 Add a greeting to the central rectangle in the centre of the card as shown.

STEP 4 Finally, cut out the shape, including the internal pop-up feature and fold all the crease lines as shown but without forming the card. Open it flat and refold, starting with the central vertical fold from A, followed by the long sections which form the upper and lower flaps, and then the central horizontal fold, to finally encapsulate the inner text section.

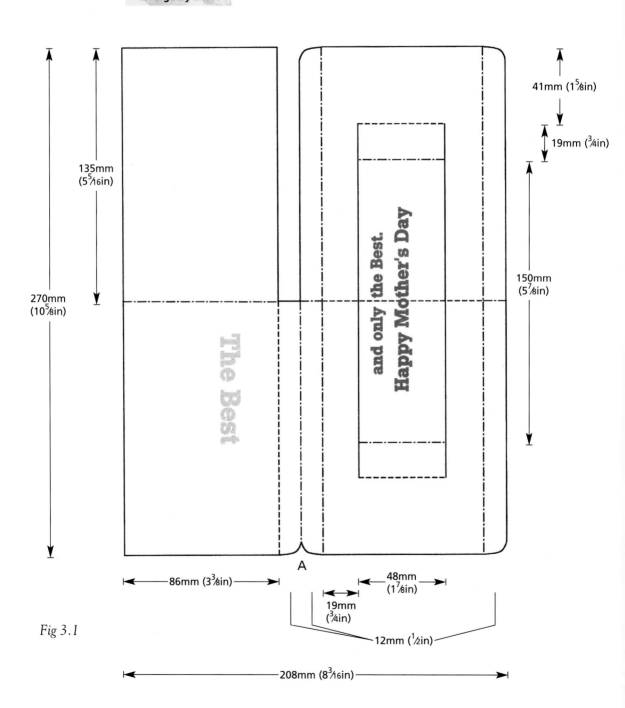

Enlarge by 200%

41mm (1⅝in)

19mm (¾in)

135mm (5⁵⁄₁₆in)

150mm (5⅞in)

270mm (10⅝in)

The Best

and only the Best.
Happy Mother's Day

A

86mm (3⅜in)

48mm (1⅞in)

19mm (¾in)

12mm (½in)

208mm (8³⁄₁₆in)

Fig 3.1

Pyramid gift box

This striking gift box features a cut out of the letter A which imitates nicely the shape of the box. The floral decoration at the top provides a feminine touch. The box contains a card platform to hold securely into place a brightly wrapped miniature bottle of perfume.

MATERIALS AND EQUIPMENT

Single A4 sheet of stiff or foil-backed card
Plain card of medium thickness, 102 x 63mm (4 x 2½in) (for the platform)
Multipurpose adhesive
Clear adhesive tape
Craft or trimming knife
Metal-edged ruler
Scoring tool

METHOD

STEP 1 Transfer the pattern onto the card (see Fig 3.2, facing opposite).

STEP 2 Cut out the letter and then around the outside edge of the shape, leaving the flowers at the top until last.

STEP 3 Where marked, score the crease lines on the interior and then fold.

STEP 4 Glue the side tab (A). Once dry, glue the top flap (B), using a long utensil (the end of a pencil is ideal) to hold the tab in place while it dries.

STEP 5 Next, construct the card platform to hold the gift in place (see Fig 3.3, page 58). For a secure fit, place the bottle on the template and draw around the base. Cut out the hole.

STEP 6 Crease along the fold lines to form the platform.

STEP 7 Wrap the bottle in coordinating tissue paper, place it into the hole in the platform and then slide it carefully inside the box.

STEP 8 Close the base flap and secure it discreetly with a small piece of tape.

STEP 9 Twist the flowers into shape over the top of the pyramid, slotting the end flowers together.

STEP 10 To make a matching gift tag, copy the letter you want to use from your template onto an off-cut of the same card. Cut out the letter and around the outside of the shape to form a gift tag, allowing sufficient space for a greeting and about 25mm (1in) extra in length at one edge to valley fold and insert into the base of the box.

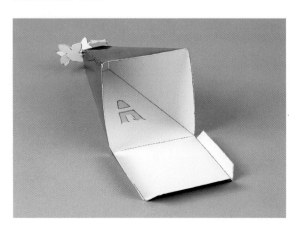

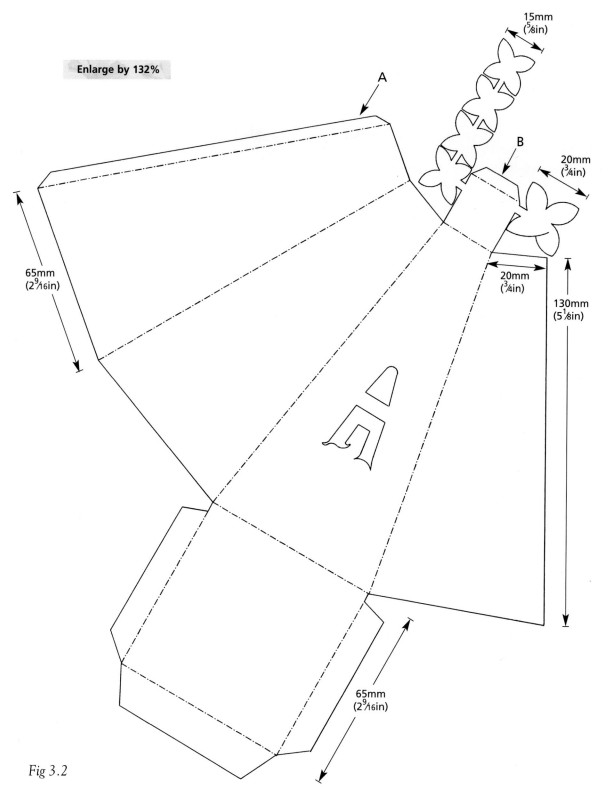

Enlarge by 132%

A

B

15mm
($\frac{5}{8}$in)

20mm
($\frac{3}{4}$in)

65mm
(2$\frac{9}{16}$in)

20mm
($\frac{3}{4}$in)

130mm
(5$\frac{1}{8}$in)

65mm
(2$\frac{9}{16}$in)

Fig 3.2

Actual size

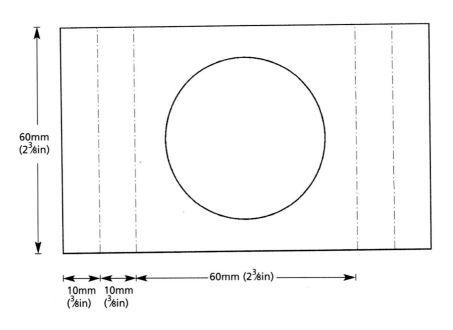

60mm
(2³⁄₈in)

10mm   10mm
(³⁄₈in)   (³⁄₈in)

60mm (2³⁄₈in)

Fig 3.3

Christmas cactus display

The flowering blooms of this Christmas cactus design drape naturally over the gold paper vase to glorious effect.

MATERIALS AND EQUIPMENT

VASE
Sheet of thin card, 305mm (12in) square (to make a vase 95mm (3¾in) in height)

SINGLE CACTUS STEM
Two sheets of A4 green card
Single sheet of A4 pink card
Strip of white paper, 178 x 50mm (7 x 2in)
Paints (red, yellow and white)
Paintbrush
Pencil
Metal-edged ruler
Trimming knife
Scissors
Multipurpose adhesive

METHOD

STEP 1 First you need to make the vase. First enlarge the template (see Fig 3.4, page 62) on the photocopier to achieve the original size, and transfer the pattern from the template onto the square sheet of card. Score the folds as marked and then carefully cut out the vase.

STEP 2 Glue the sides of the cut-out vase together, working from the base of the vase up the edges to the top.

STEP 3 Next, work on the cactus. Following the template (see Fig 3.5a, page 63), cut two identical stems from the sheet of green card and glue together, leaving a small gap in the opening at the top and at the ends of two other sections. This is to insert the cactus flowers.

STEP 4 To form the ovary, cut out three of the small polygon shapes from the template (see Fig 3.5b, page 63). Curve each of these into cone shapes for the ovary and glue.

STEP 5 Next, cut out the petals from the pink card (see Fig 3.5c, page 63) – two layers for each flower. Paint extra colour and details onto the petals. Make a small cross-shaped cut in the centre of the petal layers where they will later be joined to the stems. Curl the petals into natural shapes.

STEP 6 Make the stamens from three pieces of white paper (see Fig 3.5d, page 63). Paint both sides of the stamens' tips red and yellow, and cut along the thin lines to separate the stamens. Apply glue to the tab at the base of the stamens and curl tightly into a round.

STEP 7 Using the multipurpose adhesive, place a small dab of glue over the cross cuts you made in each of the petals, around the base of the stamens and inside the cone shape. Insert the stamens through the hole of the cross cut and into the cone.

STEP 8 Once dry, glue the cone into the top of the cactus stem. Repeat the method with the remaining flowers.

STEP 9 Buds and other details can be painted on the stem for realism.

Enlarge by 200%

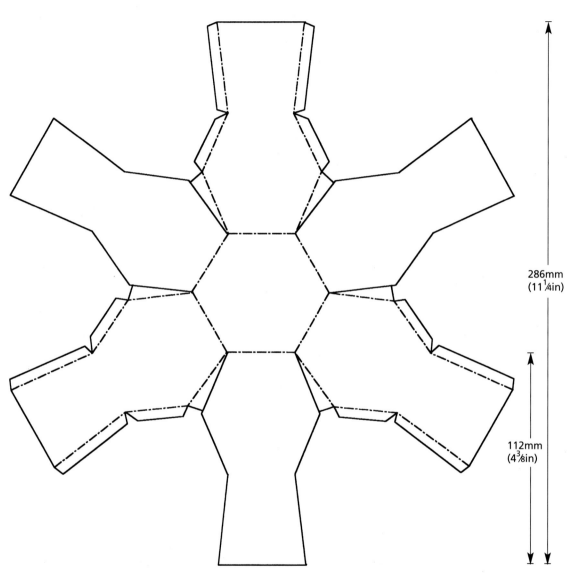

286mm
(11¼in)

112mm
(4⅜in)

Fig 3.4

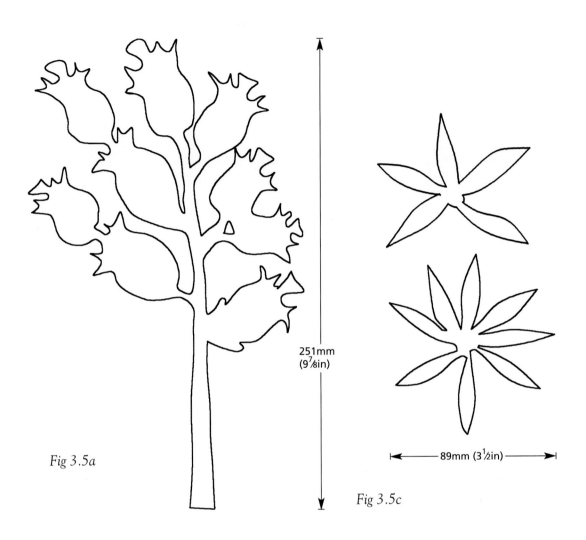

Fig 3.5a

251mm
(9$\frac{7}{8}$in)

Fig 3.5c

←— 89mm (3$\frac{1}{2}$in) —→

Enlarge all by 200%

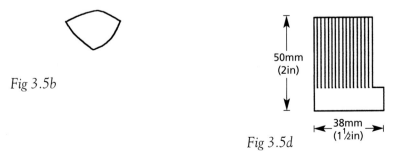

Fig 3.5b

Fig 3.5d

50mm
(2in)

←— 38mm —→
(1$\frac{1}{2}$in)

Poke napkin centrepiece

Why the name 'poke'? This is because the completed shape is reminiscent of two wee 'pokes' – an old Scottish word meaning bag. It also refers to the way napkins are poked neatly into their napkin holders. Complete as many of these as you like for a Mother's Day lunch party.

MATERIALS AND EQUIPMENT

NAPKINS

Paper napkins, standard size (one for the centrepiece and one per guest)

NAPKIN HOLDERS

Strips of card, two light green and two dark green, 838 x 50mm (33 x 2in)
Watercolour paints, light and dark green (or diluted green food colouring)
Single paper plate, 229mm (9in) in diameter
Short length of wood dowel, 25mm (1in)
Paintbrush
Clear adhesive tape
Long ruler, 457mm (18in) (optional)
Multipurpose adhesive

METHOD

STEP 1 Start by converting the square napkin into a rectangular shape. With the napkin opened out flat, make a small mark on the edge of the left- and right-hand sides, 133mm (5¼in) from the top edge. Bring up the lower edge of the napkin to meet these marks, so that you now have a rectangular shape.

STEP 2 Crease along the fold line. As you work, use a ruler to provide tension along the fold lines and to ensure a smooth, precise crease.

STEP 3 You are now ready to fold the napkin into shape. Follow diagrams 1–10 (see Fig 3.6, page 67), which are not to scale, noting that the fold lines already creased are signified on the diagram by blue, and that the looping arrow indicates to turn the work over. Fold and open the napkin twice in 1 and 2, turn it over and then crease along the diagonal in 3. Turn it over again to reach 4 where you

collapse the napkin in one movement, following A, B, C and D to form the required shape in 5. To do this, bend down A, poking it in the diagonal which will bring B across towards the left. By pushing inside the diagonal on the right, C and D will coincide at the same corner – D underneath C. Valley fold and then tuck the flap into the side pocket at 5. Turn the napkin over and similarly fold in the flap at 6. At 7, hold the lower right-hand corner, poke a finger into the left side, open it, then squash flat, to form 8. Turn it over, and at 9, form a similar poke to reach the shape shown in 10.

STEP 4 Next, make the napkin holder. Tape together the two strips of light green card to form a long length. Repeat this with the two strips of dark green card. Use them to make a concertina length as you did to make the seed heads for the sunflower centrepiece (see page 29).

STEP 5 Form the concertina paper strip into a round, ensuring that the taped edges are invisible on the inside and underneath so that it looks neat and tidy.

STEP 6 Cut off the excess card at the lower edge. Valley fold the excess card at the other end to act as a tab. Apply glue to this tab, then insert it in the slit at the alternate end to join the concertina together.

STEP 7 Gently position the piece of wood dowelling into the centre of the concertina to provide shape and support to the piece while you work the rest of the steps.

STEP 8 Apply glue to the bottom of the concertina and stick it to the centre of the paper plate.

STEP 9 With your plain paper plate, paint whatever pattern you wish around the edge in complementary colours. This part is good fun for children planning a surprise for mum to experiment with shapes and colours.

STEP 10 Remove the piece of dowel. For the centrepiece display, add a spot of glue to the gap in the centre and insert the napkin to secure. Poke the guests' folded napkins around the central napkin (without gluing), ready to use.

Not to scale

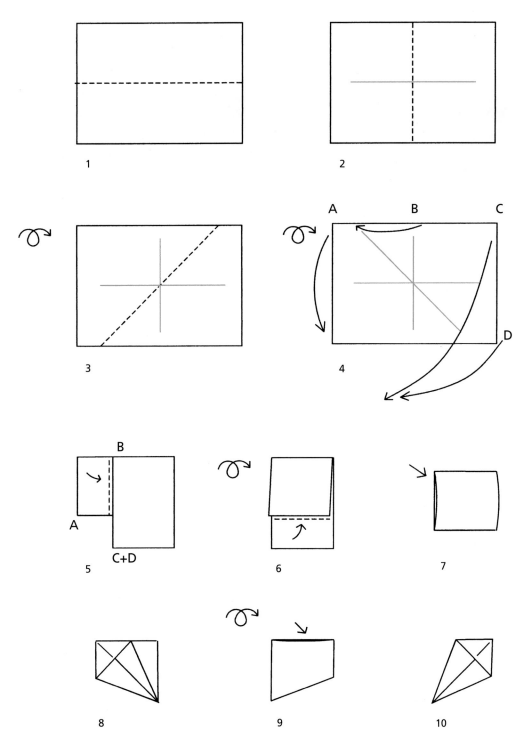

Fig 3.6

Easter

Three-dimensional Easter card

Lantern egg gift box

Easter mobile

Ring of daisies centrepiece

Three-dimensional
Easter card

This unusual card makes use of different folding techniques for a unique greeting. You have the option of completing the design on the computer or illustrating it by hand. Elaborate on my design with your own borders and motifs if you wish.

MATERIALS AND EQUIPMENT

Two sheets of different-coloured paper or thin card, 297 x 127mm (11¹¹⁄₁₆ x 5in)
Piece of card, 241 x 152mm (9½ x 6in) (for the front and back of the card)
Pencil
Metal-edged ruler
Craft knife
Scissors
Scoring tool
Multipurpose adhesive
Colouring pens, pencils or paints (optional)

METHOD

STEP 1 Transfer the template (see Fig 4.1, overleaf) onto the paper or thin card. Add your lettering to the templates. I have executed my design on the computer which you can try, too, adding each 35mm (1⅜in) high letter individually to the two templates, positioning them about 4mm (⁵⁄₃₂in) above the edge of the paper. Freehand decoration is just as effective and may free you up to use a more flexible style. The size of the finished card is 152 x 121mm (6 x 4¾in), so on the right-hand half of the piece of card, add your own design to decorate the front.

STEP 2 Cut out the templates, taking care with the scalloped edges – scissors may be best for this task.

STEP 3 Score and then fold along the lines.

STEP 4 Interlock where necessary so that both templates fit together. Fold to form a flat concertina shape.

STEP 5 Next, turn over the card to show the inside and draw a line 100mm (3¹⁵⁄₁₆in) long, beginning 20mm (¾in) from the bottom edge and 25mm (1in) in from the right-hand edge.

STEP 6 Score a line down the centre of the card and fold.

STEP 7 Take the concertina shape and check that the back of it is facing you by fanning it from left to right. It should open out with the side showing the letters visible. Close it with the back uppermost, and apply glue to the two strips of paper making up this end section.

Turn it over and glue it to the card so that the right-hand edge just covers the pencil line. Apply glue to the end sections of the paper now facing you, fold the front of the card on top and press down to ensure a secure join.

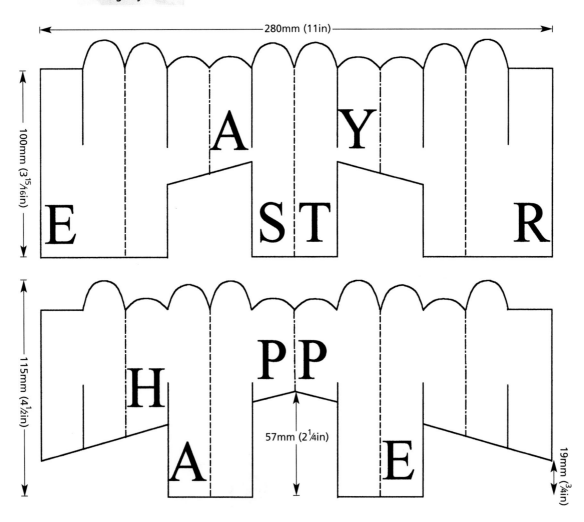

Enlarge by 200%

Fig 4.1

Lantern egg gift box

This is a useful and attractive design for presenting an Easter egg to to someone special, and afterwards, to store cherished items inside and decorate with your favourite family photos in the frames at the front of the lantern.

MATERIALS AND EQUIPMENT

A1 sheet of pale yellow card
A2 sheet of pale yellow card
A2 sheet of thin green card
Sheet of paper or thin card, 102 x 152mm (4 x 6in)
(desired colour to fit design)
Pencil
Metal-edged ruler
Trimming knife
Scoring tool
Compass
Multipurpose adhesive

METHOD

STEP 1   First enlarge all the templates for the lantern, which are a quarter of the original size, on the photocopier. Transfer the template (see Fig 4.2a, page 76) onto the A1 sheet of yellow card.

STEP 2   Score the fold lines.

STEP 3   Cut out and form the box into shape, gluing the base and side.

STEP 4   Using the template (see Fig 4.2b, page 76) as a guide for dimensions, copy the template showing the ivy leaves (see Fig 4.2c, page 77) onto the green card or draw your own freehand, making sure they approximate the guidelines.

STEP 5   Cut out the strips of ivy and fold where necessary to bend at the corners of the lantern.

STEP 6   On the reverse of the ivy, apply glue to the folds on either side of the central rectangular panel, to the inner edge at the sides and a line below the lower edge of the rectangles, thus leaving clearance for the insertion of photos in the three illustration panels at a later stage.

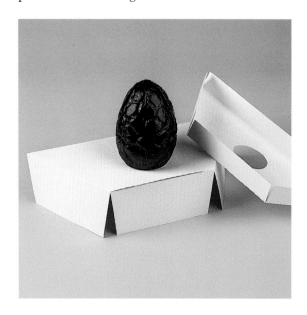

STEP 7 Design your Easter greeting on the piece of paper or thin card in a coordinating colour of your choice and slide it behind the ivy frame at the front of the lantern.

STEP 8 Transfer the template (see Fig 4.2d, page 77) to the A2 sheet of pale yellow card. This forms the platform that secures the top of the Easter egg once inserted into the lantern egg box. Because the sizes of eggs vary, test and adjust the measurement of your hole. Score the folds and cut out.

STEP 9 To make the base platform that holds the bottom of the egg, follow the same method, but extend the length of the tabs on the sides, back and front to 57mm (2¼in). Again, score the folds and cut out.

STEP 10 Cut two strips of card, 44 x 10mm (1¾ x ⅜in), glue together and then across the inside top of the box back, 29mm (1⅛in) down from the central point. This ensures the lantern lid maintains its shape and is not pushed down too far.

STEP 11 Fill the area beneath the base platform with sweets, insert the platform above it, then the egg into the hole and finally, invert the top platform and insert it.

STEP 12 Hold the lid sections of the Easter lantern in place with the ivy, manipulating the centre piece of ivy first and then fold over and join the side pieces of ivy, cutting a small slit in each where necessary to slot them neatly together.

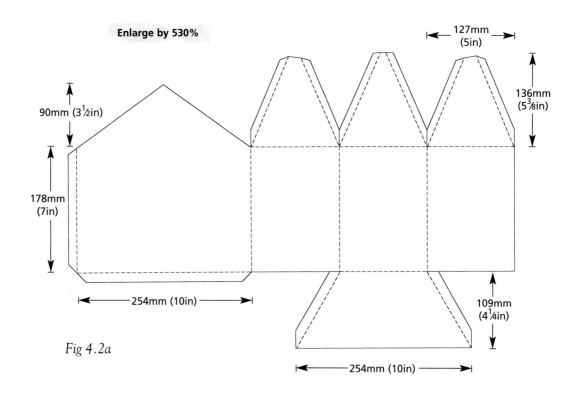

Enlarge by 530%

127mm
(5in)

136mm
(5³⁄₈in)

90mm (3½in)

178mm
(7in)

254mm (10in)

109mm
(4¼in)

Fig 4.2a

254mm (10in)

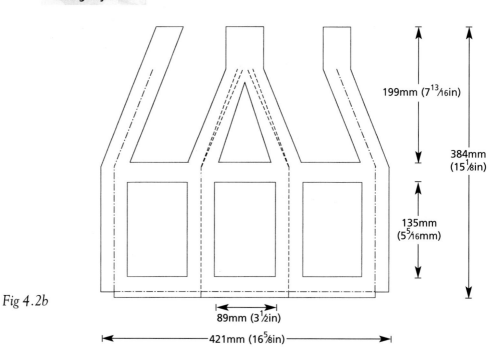

Enlarge by 530%

199mm (7¹³⁄₁₆in)

384mm
(15⅛in)

135mm
(5⁵⁄₁₆mm)

Fig 4.2b

89mm (3½in)

421mm (16⅝in)

Enlarge by 406%

Fig 4.2c

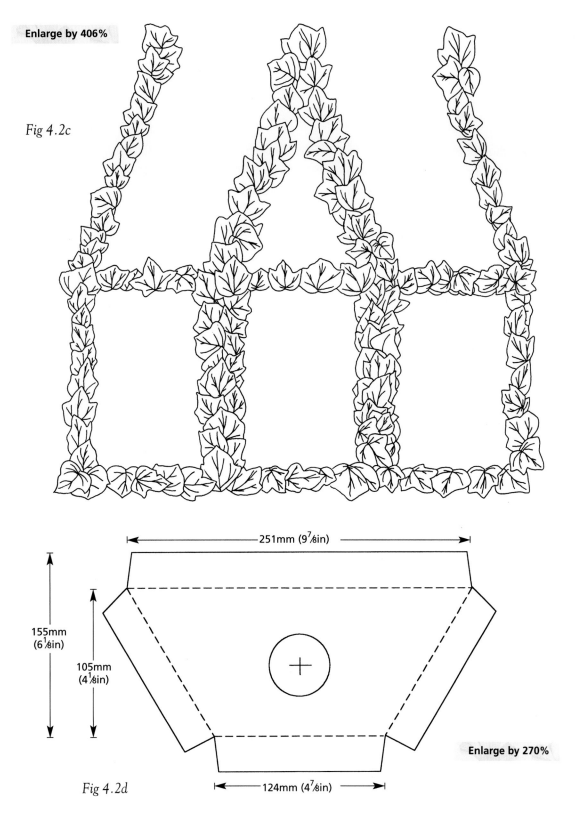

251mm (9⅞in)

155mm
(6⅛in)

105mm
(4⅛in)

+

Enlarge by 270%

Fig 4.2d

124mm (4⅞in)

Easter mobile

This mobile is a great feature for spring: flowering forsythia, little spring pansies and fresh green leaves. To complement the mobile – and for extra impact – make one or two additional branches to display upright in a vase.

MATERIALS AND EQUIPMENT

Sheet of yellow tissue paper, 264 x 114mm (10⅜ x 4½in)
Roll of brown corrugated card
Sheet of green card, 210 x 102mm (8¼ x 4in)
Sheet of mauve card, 178 x 229mm (7 x 9in)
Sheet of purple card, 191 x 105mm (7½ x 4⅛in)
Yellow paint
Paintbrush
Black felt-tip pen (or black paint and fine-tipped brush)
Nylon thread
Length of green embroidery cotton
Needle
20 small rubber bands
Length of wood dowelling, 700mm (27½in) long, 10mm (⅜in) in diameter
Craft knife
Metal-edged ruler
Pair of scissors
Stick and multipurpose adhesives
Compass
Pencil

METHOD

STEP 1 Cut the tissue paper into 12 same-sized rectangles, each 44 x 57mm (1¾ x 2¼in). These will form the forsythia petals.

STEP 2 Fold each same-sized rectangle in half lengthways twice.

STEP 3 Cut out a petal shape from one end of this long strip (see Fig 4.3a, page 81).

STEP 4 Bend down the two outer petals and then twist the others to radiate from the centre.

STEP 5   Fold the stalk in half again lengthways to make it narrower.

STEP 6   Turn to the branch itself. Take the corrugated card and cut to the following dimensions: 86 x 700mm (3⅜ x 27½in). Firmly roll the corrugated card around the length of wood dowelling to shape it.

STEP 7   Unroll it again, make a few small slits where you would like your flowers and leaves to be inserted, keeping them within a 50mm (2in) lengthways strip, measured from the outer edge. Insert and glue some of the flowers as appropriate.

STEP 8   Carefully roll up the card to avoid crushing the flowers, add glue and the remaining flowers to the edge and slide rubber bands carefully over them to secure the 'branch' while it dries.

STEP 9   Once dry, cut off the bands.

STEP 10   Transfer the leaf templates onto the green card (see Figs 4.3b and 4.3c, opposite).

STEP 11   Add the hatching lines as shown, using a black pen or some paint applied with a fine-tipped brush, then cut out and gently crease each leaf into shape.

STEP 12   Glue the leaves together and then to the branch.

STEP 13   Make copies of each of the pansy templates (see Figs 4.3d and 4.3e, opposite) – 12 copies of Fig 4.3d on the mauve card and 12 copies of Fig 4.3e on the purple card.

STEP 14   Paint yellow centres on the mauve petals, and some black lines for detail. If you have a reference for this, it is very helpful.

STEP 15   Cut out the pansies. Fold along the tiny lines shown (see Fig 4.3e).

STEP 16   For each pansy, glue A and B under the central petal on the first template and then glue the second template to the back.

STEP 17   Once complete, thread a needle, attach the flowers together in groups of four with the green embroidery cotton to make three bunches, securing them with discrete knots across the folded section and then mount to the branch.

STEP 18   Finally, add a length of nylon thread to the branch to suspend at a natural angle.

All actual size

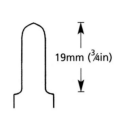

19mm (¾in)

Fig 4.3a

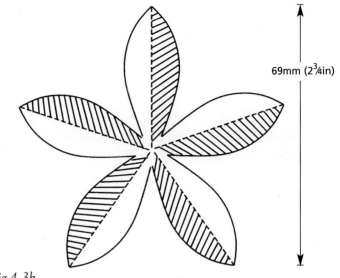

69mm (2¾in)

Fig 4.3b

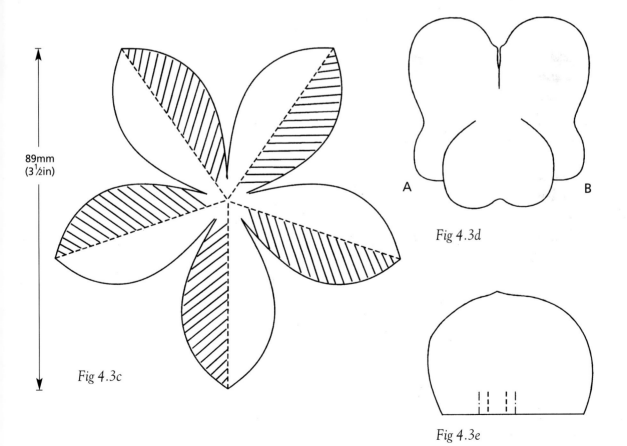

89mm
(3½in)

Fig 4.3c

A   B

Fig 4.3d

Fig 4.3e

Ring of daisies centrepiece

A delicate daisy chain was the inspiration for this design. As a table centrepiece, scatter extra cut-out daisies over the tablecloth. Alternatively, you might like to convert it into a mobile and suspend it from the ceiling with some extra thread.

MATERIALS AND EQUIPMENT

A1 sheet of medium thick cream card
A4 sheet of green card
Six A4 sheets of white paper
Compass
Craft knife or pair of scissors
Watercolour paint in yellow, red and green
Black felt-tip pen
Stick adhesive
Nylon thread and needle

METHOD

STEP 1 Enlarge the first template (see Fig 4.4, overleaf) to the original size. The second template (see Fig 4.5, page 85) also needs to be enlarged. Transfer the templates onto the sheets of cream and green card, then cut out.

STEP 2 Take a sheet of white paper, fold in half widthways, then lengthways, and again widthways until you have eight equal sections.

STEP 3 Draw a circle, radius 25mm (1in), on the top section. Cut around the circle through all eight layers and then cut a scalloped edge to each circle like petals.

STEP 4 Repeat the above method on the remaining sheets of paper to make a total of 48 daisies.

STEP 5 Paint 24 of the daisies with a green circle on the back of the daisies and, on the remaining half, a yellow circle for the front of the flowers.

STEP 6 Add red paint to the tips of some of the daisies and a few black dots to the yellow centres for realism.

STEP 7 Next, make a small hole in the base of the stem section to accommodate the thread and a hole at the end of each stem, as marked in the template (see Fig 4.4).

STEP 8 Turn to the cream strips of card that you will make into a 'globe'. Glue the backs of the daisies to what will become the inside of the globe, two per strip.

STEP 9 Turn over the cream card and glue the daisy fronts into position.

STEP 10 Tie a good-sized knot into the nylon thread, thread the needle and pass it through the base from the outside. Securely glue two daisies onto the thread, bearing in mind the thread will be about 127mm (5in) in length once the globe is complete.

STEP 11 Gently bend over the strips in opposite pairs, passing the thread through the holes, and ensuring it does not catch on the petals. Secure with a firm knot.

STEP 12 Glue the green leaf section (see Fig 4.5) to the base of the globe and attach a single daisy to the top of the globe to obscure the knots at either end.

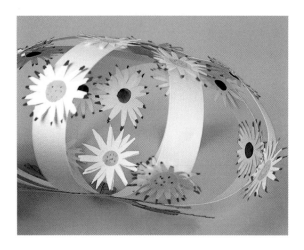

Enlarge by 530%

594mm (23$\frac{3}{8}$in)

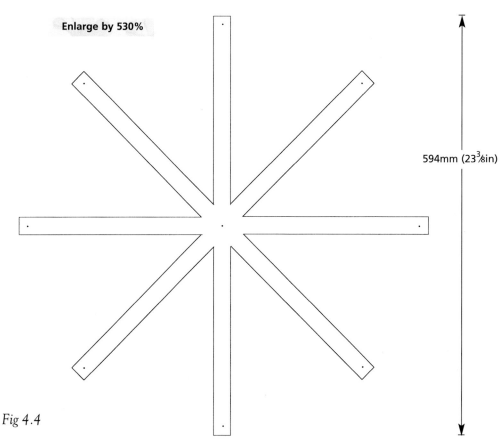

Fig 4.4

Enlarge by 132%

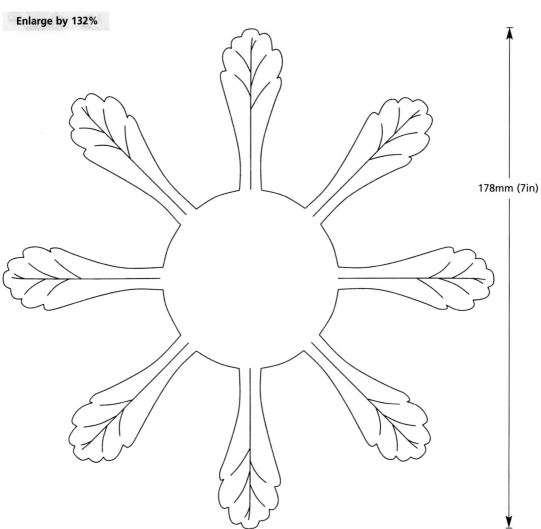

178mm (7in)

Fig 4.5

Father's Day

Castellated card

Star-shaped gift box

Sun god decoration

Geometric boxes

Castellated card

This stunning silver-foil card will be a lovely surprise for dad on Father's Day.
It looks complex, but don't worry, it is simply a matter of folding it correctly.

MATERIALS AND EQUIPMENT

Single A4 sheet of foil-backed card (desired colour)
Trimming knife
Scoring tool
Metal-edged ruler

METHOD

STEP 1 First enlarge the template (see Fig 5.1, overleaf) to match the original scale, then transfer the pattern onto the foil-backed card.

STEP 2 Turn to the reverse side of the card, and score the fold lines where indicated.

STEP 3 Cut around the outside edge, then cut out the row of squares and the other inner cut lines as marked.

STEP 4 Again, on the reverse, begin folding at the lowest edge and work upwards.

STEP 5 Return to the front of the card and crease all the folds, starting with what will be the bottom edge of the back section.

STEP 6 Once all the folds are complete and your castellated card stands alone, write your greetings on the reverse.

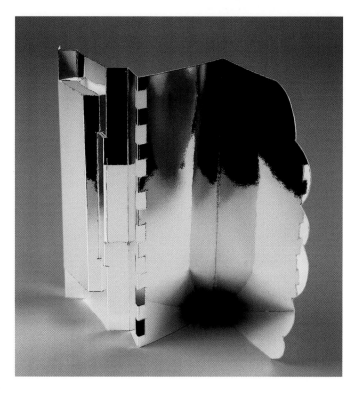

Enlarge by 200%

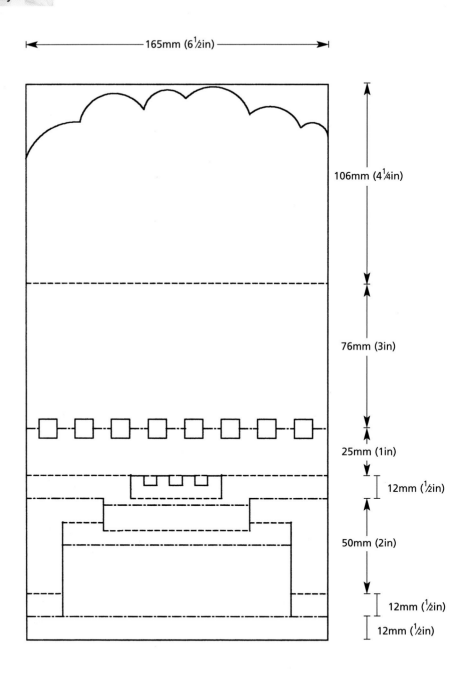

|← —————— 165mm (6½in) —————— →|

106mm (4¼in)

76mm (3in)

25mm (1in)

12mm (½in)

50mm (2in)

12mm (½in)

12mm (½in)

Fig 5.1

Star-shaped gift box

For the father with a fascination for science fiction, this is a really fun gift box to make, with its striking, geometric design and pop-off lid.

MATERIALS AND EQUIPMENT

Two sheets of A4 card (to make a box 127mm (5in) tall)
Pencil
Metal-edged ruler
Trimming knife
Multipurpose adhesive

METHOD

STEP 1 Transfer the templates (see Fig 5.2, facing opposite and pages 94–95) onto the back of your foil-backed card. Cut out the five parts that make up the box.

STEP 2 Take the cut out for Fig 5.2a, the 'collar' for the lid of the box, and bend it gently into a curve, overlapping the two ends by 6mm (¼in). Glue the overlap to join the ends.

STEP 3 Repeat this method with Fig 5.2b to form the body of the gift box.

STEP 4 Turn to Fig 5.2c. Score the circle at the base where the circle meets the ring of triangles, then bend the tabs, apply glue to the outer edge and insert into the base of the box body. Hold the tabs firmly in place until dry. Use the flat end of a pencil to help you.

STEP 5 Next, make the star-shaped lid. First score the top section of the lid (see Fig 5.2d) and crease as shown, starting with the folds near the centre and working outwards. Avoid the tip at the centre – this is a weak point and the lines converge here to form a natural point anyway.

STEP 6 Glue the parts marked A together and then the corresponding sections as shown to form the star shape.

STEP 7 Slide the collar section into the lid. Stick the tab marked B and the corresponding sections at equal distances around the top edge of the collar.

STEP 8 Next, form the lower section of the star-shaped lid (see Fig 5.2e). Score the central circle and then along the edge of the star shape. Fold the triangular sections around the edge.

STEP 9 Bend the tabs in the centre and slide the lid into the collar, aligning the points of the star.

STEP 10 Take the multipurpose adhesive and add a dab of glue to the edge tabs to form the enclosed star.

STEP 11 Add another dab of glue to each of the central tabs to hold them against the collar of the lid.

Father's Day

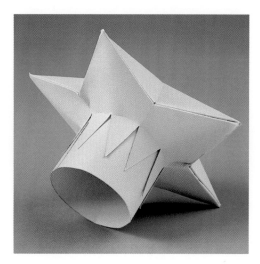

Enlarge by 132%

Lid collar

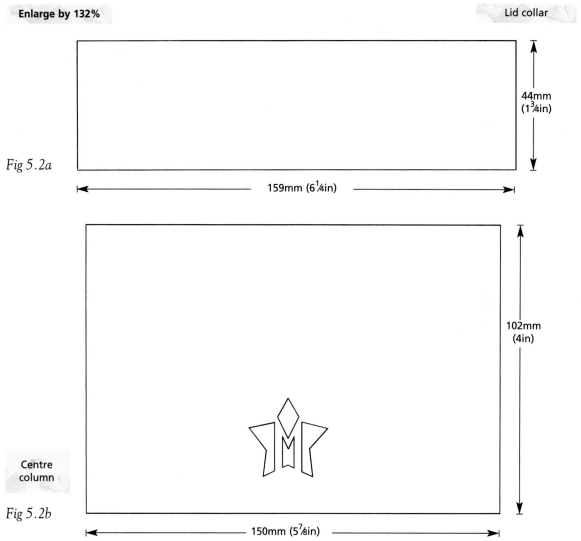

Fig 5.2a

44mm
(1¾in)

← 159mm (6¼in) →

Centre
column

Fig 5.2b

102mm
(4in)

← 150mm (5⅞in) →

Enlarge both by 132%

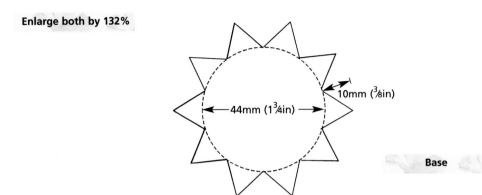

10mm (⅜in)

44mm (1¾in)

Base

Fig 5.2c

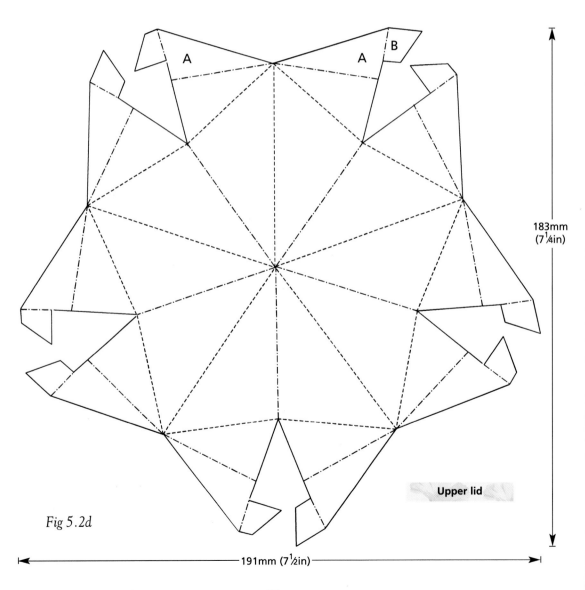

A

A

B

183mm
(7¼in)

Upper lid

Fig 5.2d

191mm (7½in)

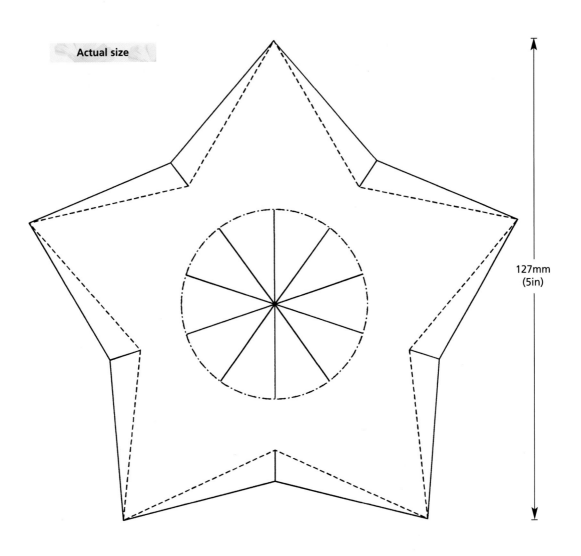

Actual size

127mm
(5in)

Fig 5.2e

Lower lid

95

Sun god decoration

This sun god is a fiery fellow – and he looks very impressive once mounted
to a wall or a window.

MATERIALS AND EQUIPMENT

Single A4 sheet of thin, gold foil-backed card
Single A4 sheet each of orange, red and mid-brown
Scrap of white paper (or white paint)
Pair of scissors
Craft knife
Nylon thread

METHOD

STEP 1 First enlarge and then transfer the templates (see Fig 5.3, pages 98–99) onto the sheets of coloured card to form four layers.

STEP 2 Cut out the four layers, including the eye sockets in Fig 5.3a, the large central holes in Figs 5.3b and 5.3c and, if using paper for the eyes, the eye sockets – but not the iris in Fig 5.3d.

STEP 3 Glue a scrap of white paper behind the eyes in Fig 5.3d or use white paint for the whites of the eyes.

STEP 4 Join Figs 5.3b and 5.3c together, by bringing the parts labelled A to D (see Fig 5.3c) to overlap the clumps of hair in the layer above it (see Fig 5.3b).

STEP 5 Place the first layer (Fig 5.3a) on top of the layers just joined to form three layers.

STEP 6 Take what will be the bottom layer (Fig 5.3d) and roll the moustache lengthwise, both parts together, starting with the tips. Pass this from the back of the third layer through the second layer and the hole in the top layer. Reform the moustache as necessary.

STEP 7 Turn to the reverse of the project and slip the eyebrow hairs through the slits in what will be the top layer once complete, and then bend them at an angle to form the eyebrows.

STEP 8 Shape the nose outwards slightly to give it a bit of form.

STEP 9 Attach a short length of nylon thread to the two small parallel slits at the top of the head (see Fig 5.3d) and suspend it where desired – from a window, shelf or ceiling.

Enlarge all by 182%

157mm (6$\frac{3}{16}$in)

165mm
(6$\frac{1}{2}$in)

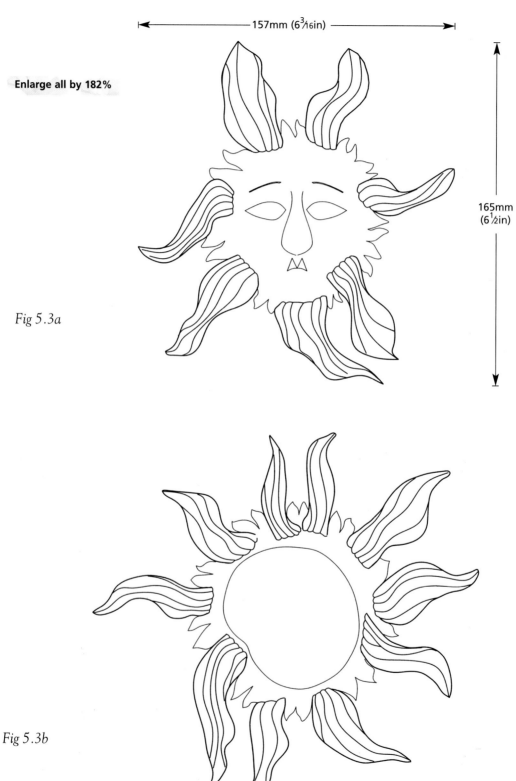

Fig 5.3a

Fig 5.3b

A

D

C

B

Fig 5.3c

Fig 5.3d

Geometric boxes

These small boxes are based on mathematical shapes which can be decoratively arranged in the centre of the dining table for dad's celebratory dinner. Use silver foil-backed card for the boxes and have them strewn with metallic ribbons, or add patterns to the card prior to cutting out. If you wish, you can increase the dimensions for a distinctive display.

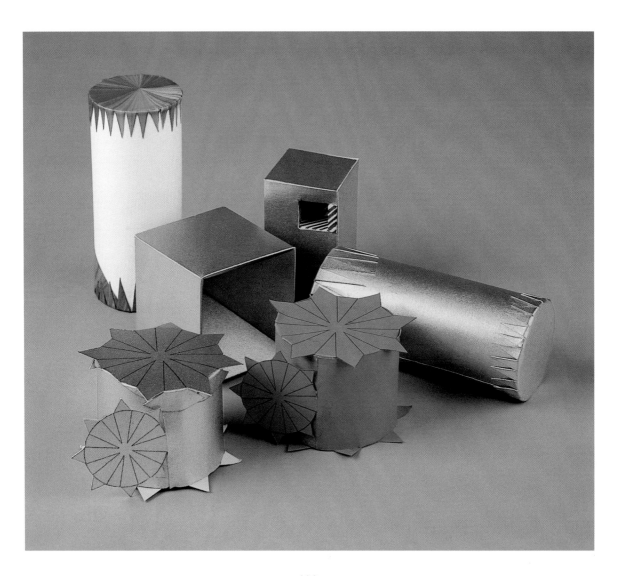

MATERIALS AND EQUIPMENT

EACH BOX
A4 sheet of foil-backed or coloured card
Pencil
Scoring tool
Metal-edged ruler
Trimming knife
Multipurpose adhesive
Rubber bands/clothes pegs/tweezers
Paint (optional)

PYRAMID IN A SQUARE

METHOD

STEP 1 Transfer the template (see Fig 5.4a, page 104) onto your chosen card. Score all fold lines on the back of the card to avoid any visible lines. Cut-score the fold for the box lid.

STEP 2 Cut around the outside edge of the box.

STEP 3 Glue the box together, starting with the pyramid shape and then the side of the cube. Use tweezers to help ensure the tabs of the pyramid hold together while the glue dries. And, if you are working quickly, use two clothes pegs per join while the glue sets.

STEP 4 Finally, stick the lid in place.

STEP 5 For a bigger box, enlarge the dimensions throughout, although the triangular sections will need a smaller increase in the length from base to apex, to allow room inside the box for the present.

SQUARE IN RECTANGLE

METHOD

STEP 1 Transfer the template (see Fig 5.4b, page 105) to the card, score the fold lines and then cut out.

STEP 2 If you prefer the square to be decorative, turn the card over so that what will be the interior of the box is visible and colour in the five faces of the square section.

STEP 3 Turn the card over. Crease all the folds and then pass what will be the square through the cut-out section.

STEP 4 Glue the square and then stick it to the side of the rectangle. Use rubber bands to help hold it together while it dries.

STEP 5 Finally, form the rectangular box by gluing the tabs in alphabetical order, starting at A. Use the photo, below left, as a guide.

STEP 6 If you wish, add a gift tag to a larger version of this box by inserting the thread of the tag through the gap between the two layers of card at the edge of the square section.

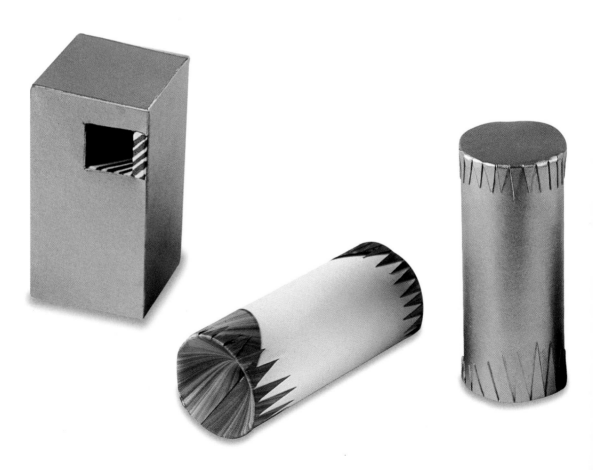

CONE IN CYLINDER

METHOD

STEP 1 Transfer the template (see Fig 5.4c, page 106) onto the card, and carefully cut out the shape.

STEP 2 Curve the cylinder section. To do this, roll it round a tube shape as a guide. The diameter should measure 48mm (1⅞in). Glue the tab. Next, make up the box. Use the photo, opposite bottom right as a guide.

STEP 3 First, form the cone section of the box by curving the card and applying glue to the overlapping tab.

STEP 4 Fold the triangular tabs and stick on the side of the cylinder.

STEP 5 Similarly, glue the tabs at the other end of the cylinder.

WHEEL

METHOD

STEP 1 Transfer the template (see Fig 5.4d, page 107) to the card and cut out the shape around the outer edges. The solid, inner lines are added for decoration

STEP 2 Curve the central section, using a tube shape as a guide. The diameter should measure 58mm (2¼in). Glue the tab to form a cylinder.

STEP 3 Crease the mountain folds on wheel B and then glue these tabs inside the cylinder.

STEP 4 Repeat this step with section C – although sticking the tabs around the outside of the cylinder adds an attractive pattern to the edge.

STEP 5 Wheel A will stand out from the main cylinder shape, and can be used as a gift tag.

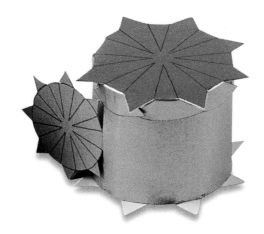

Enlarge by 132%

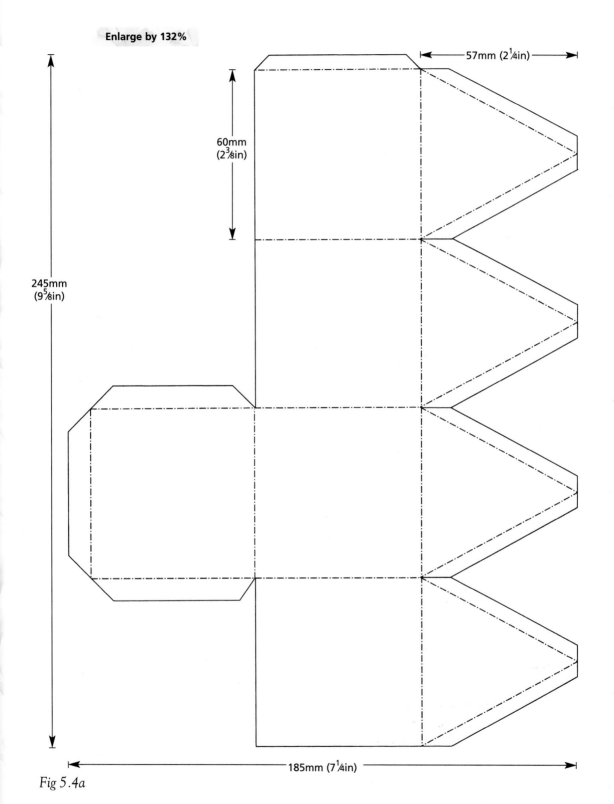

57mm (2¼in)

60mm (2⅜in)

245mm (9⅝in)

185mm (7¼in)

Fig 5.4a

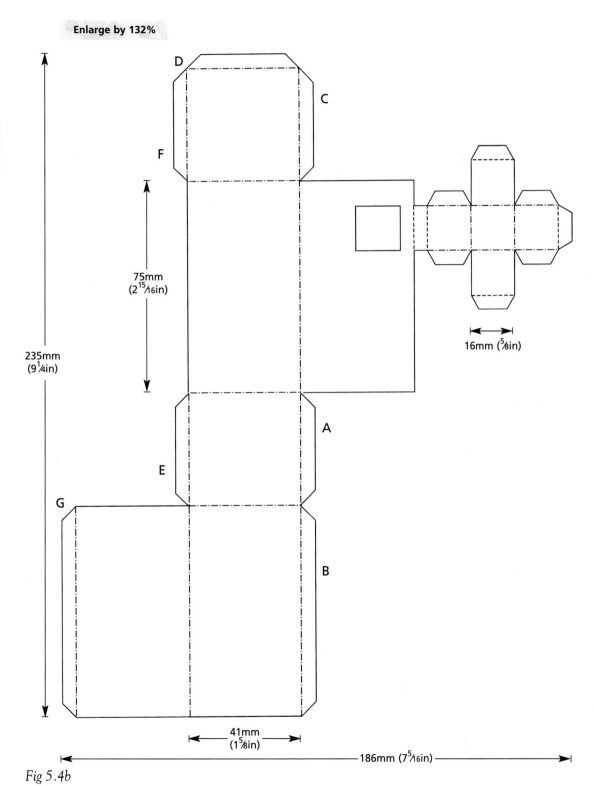

Enlarge by 132%

75mm
(2¹⁵⁄₁₆in)

235mm
(9¼in)

16mm (⅝in)

41mm
(1⅝in)

186mm (7⁵⁄₁₆in)

Fig 5.4b

Enlarge by 132%

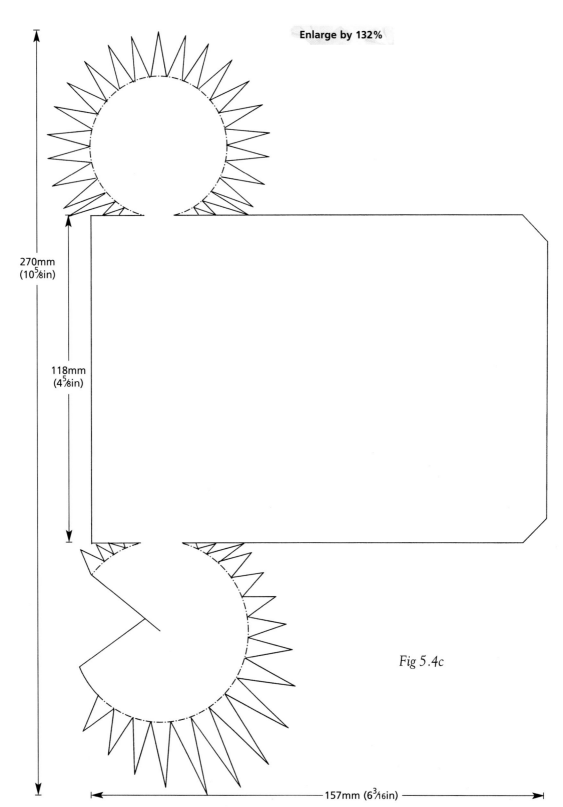

270mm
(10⅝in)

118mm
(4⅝in)

Fig 5.4c

157mm (6³⁄₁₆in)

Enlarge by 132%

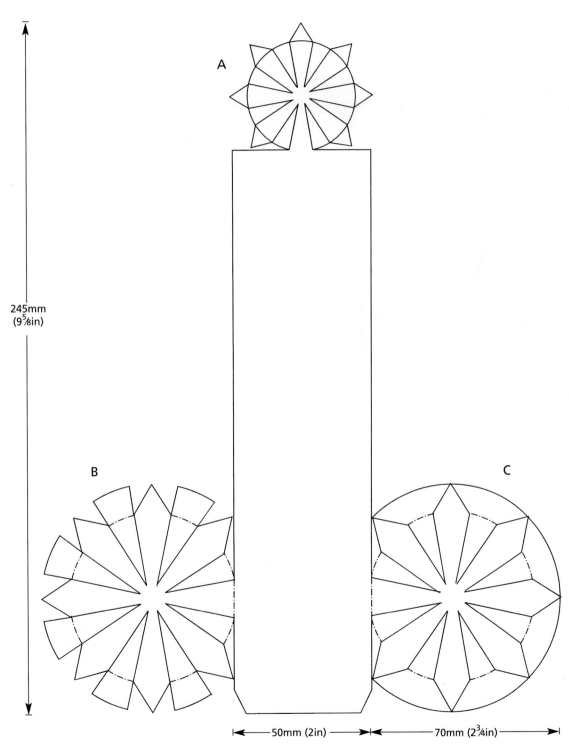

A

B

C

245mm
(9⅝in)

50mm (2in)

70mm (2¾in)

Fig 5.4d

Wedding Anniversary

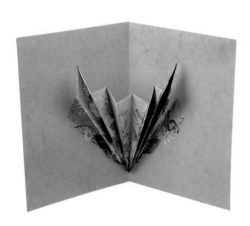

Bouquet card

Anniversary gift box

Pot-pourri plate

Floral table centrepiece

 Bouquet card

This pretty card has a vibrantly painted concertina folded on the inside to form a fan, and is decorated in a floral design with warm summer colours.

MATERIALS AND EQUIPMENT

Sheet of card, 254 x 178mm (10 x 7in)
Sheet of paper, 292 x 191mm (11½ x 7½in)
Watercolour paints
Paintbrush
Stick adhesive
Pencil
Straight edge
Craft knife

METHOD

STEP 1 First enlarge the template (see Fig 6.1, overleaf) to obtain the original size, then transfer the template onto the sheet of paper, marking where the fold lines are indicated on the template.

STEP 2 Paint a bouquet of flowers in the central pentagonal shape, using the fold lines marked around the shape as guides for the position of the flowers.

STEP 3 Carefully fold the shape so that all creases converge on the central base point at A, and then cut around the pentagon shape. Check the main photo to help guide you. Decorate the front of the card as you wish, before gluing the two side sections of the fan to the card at a 40° angle, as shown.

STEP 4 Finish the card by cutting around the edge with pinking shears (optional).

Enlarge by 265%

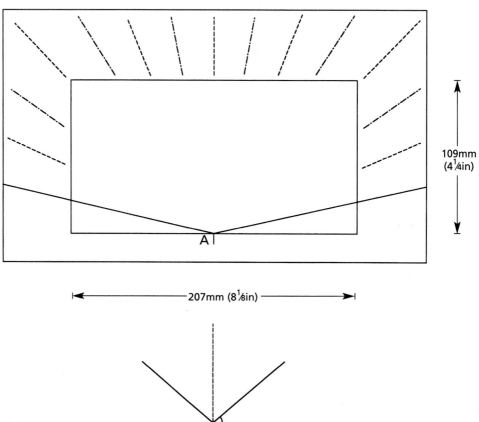

109mm
(4¼in)

207mm (8⅛in)

Fig 6.1

Anniversary gift box

This anniversary gift box is made from blue foil-backed card in honour of a sapphire wedding anniversary (45 years). Match your foil-backed card to the anniversary you wish to celebrate: silver is 25 years, pearl is 30, ruby is 40, gold is 50 and emerald is 55 years.

MATERIALS AND EQUIPMENT

Sheet of B2 foil-backed card, 500 x 707mm (19⅝ x 27⅞in)
Metal-edged ruler
Scoring tool
Trimming knife
Multipurpose adhesive

METHOD

STEP 1 This gift box will fit a gift 102mm (4in) square. First enlarge the template (see Fig 6.2, facing opposite) for the original scale and then transfer the pattern to the card.

STEP 2 Score along the fold lines, cut out the shape and write your greeting on the reverse of the gift tag, which is attached to the lid.

STEP 3 Next, crease all the folds you have scored, form the box into its pyramid shape by drawing it together at each side, glue the open sides along the edges, followed by the small top tabs. Finally, ensure that you insert your present safely inside the box and close the base, securing with a discreet piece of sticky tape.

Enlarge by 400%

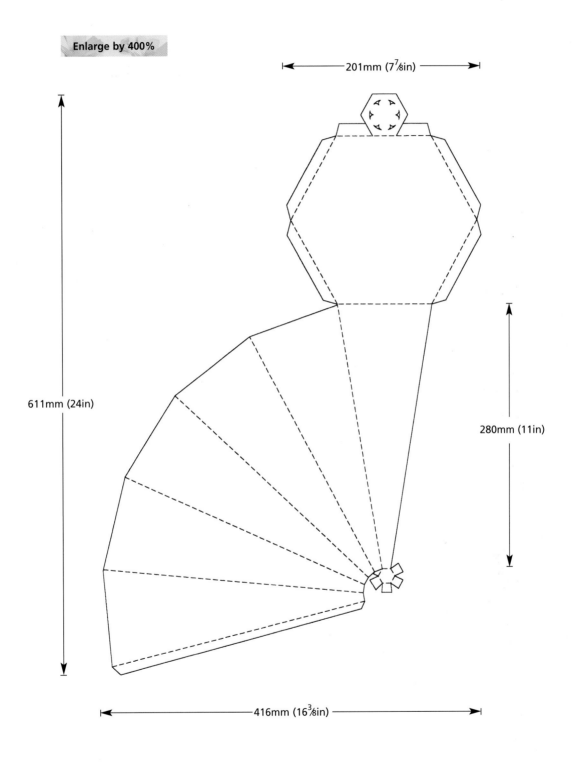

Fig 6.2

Pot-pourri plate

This is a great gift idea for the children to make for mum, dad or the grandparents. The techniques are very simple, using the minimum of glue and just a little scissor work.

MATERIALS AND EQUIPMENT

Two white paper plates, 229mm (9in) in diameter
Multipurpose adhesive
Pot-pourri (own mix as desired)
Pencil
Craft knife or safety scissors (for children)
Circular object, 140mm (5½in) in diameter

METHOD

STEP 1 Transfer the template (see Fig 6.3, below) onto the the first paper plate.

STEP 2 Cut out the pattern in the following order: the couple, inner arch, outer arc.

STEP 3 Mountain fold the design so it stands erect from the inverted plate once secure.

STEP 4 Apply glue to the edge of the second white plate and then glue the two plates facing together. You will be left with a bowl in the centre to hold the pot pourri.

STEP 5 Select your pot pourri and fill the plate. I used a rose-coloured mix, but there are many nice, fragrant alternatives.

Enlarge by 142%

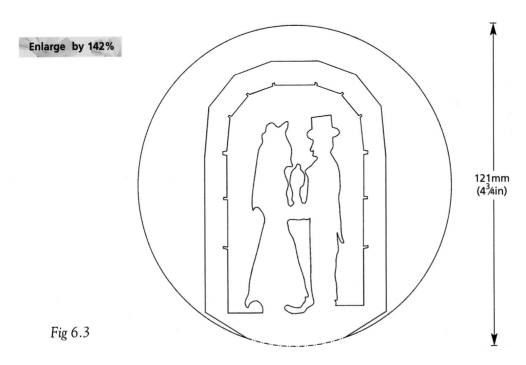

121mm
(4¾in)

Fig 6.3

Floral table centrepiece

This is another project making use of paper plates, this time combined with the folding techniques in the 'poke' napkin project (see page 64).

MATERIALS AND EQUIPMENT

Two sheets each of thin A4 card in pink, mauve, purple
Single sheet of thin A4 card in green
White paper plate, 229mm (9in) in diameter
Pencil
Metal-edged ruler
Craft or trimming knife
Multipurpose adhesive

METHOD

STEP 1 You will need five rectangles each of
pink, mauve and purple card, measuring 105 x
148mm (4⅛ x 5⅞in). You will also need three
same-sized rectangles in green card.

STEP 2 Fold these 18 rectangles of card as for
the 'poke' shape (see step 3 in the poke napkin
project and the accompanying template, Fig 3.6,
on page 67), replacing the napkin with card.

STEP 3 Glue the three green shapes, slotted
together to form a green stalk.

STEP 4 For the flowers, assemble as shown in
the photos, gluing a mauve and a purple shape
into a pink shape.

STEP 5 Glue the arrangement to the plate
and add the green stalk.

Christmas

Holy family Christmas card

Children's art gift box

Smiling Santa wall hanging

Floral yule log

Holy family Christmas card

The illustration for this design is an abstract interpretation of the holy family for a modern twist on the traditional Christmas card. Vary your own design if you wish, and create your own greetings and motifs.

MATERIALS AND EQUIPMENT

Sheet of A4 card (own choice of colour)
Pencil
Metal-edged ruler
Coloured pencils, pens or paint
Craft knife

METHOD

STEP 1 Transfer the template for the design (see Fig 7.1, overleaf) onto the card.

STEP 2 Create your design using your chosen medium to work the holy family figures, greetings text and any motifs.

STEP 3 Cut and fold as shown on the template, following the marked lines as indicated, to form the card.

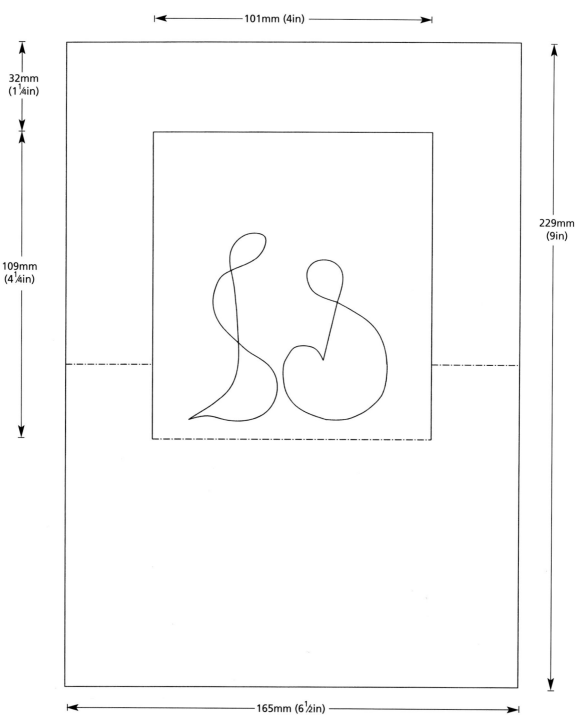

Enlarge by 132%

101mm (4in)

32mm (1¼in)

229mm (9in)

109mm (4¼in)

165mm (6½in)

Fig 7.1

Children's art gift box

This delightful Christmas gift box will be kept long after the festive season to store all kinds of useful objects – even photographs – as a charming reminder of your children's early artwork. To avoid indignant remarks from the artist – 'That's not the right way round!' – the top of the gift box is artwork-free.

MATERIALS AND EQUIPMENT

A1 sheet of thick card (foil-backed or coloured) to construct a box
178 x 152 x 127mm (7 x 6 x 5in)
Colour copies or photos of four unique pieces of artwork
Pencil
Metal-edged ruler
Trimming knife
Multipurpose adhesive

METHOD

STEP 1 First enlarge your template (see Fig 7.2, facing opposite) to match the original size and transfer it to what will be the inside of the card. Score along the inside lines to avoid marks.

STEP 2 Cut out and crease the folds – all are valley folds. Open out flat with the exterior of the card facing up.

STEP 3 Take your colour photocopies, scans or photos of your child's art and stick them into place on each side of the box, omitting the lid of the box.

STEP 4 Form the folded card into a box shape and glue the sides and the base flap, before closing the lid.

Enlarge by 400%

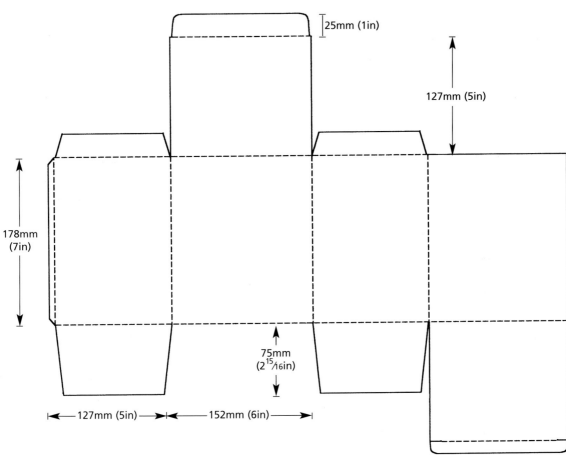

25mm (1in)

127mm (5in)

178mm
(7in)

75mm
(2^{15}/16in)

|← 127mm (5in) →|← 152mm (6in) →|

Fig 7.2

Smiling Santa wall hanging

A mass of curls topped by a red hat, this Santa decoration will add a suitably festive touch to a wall or against a window; the sunlight will shine through his eyes and add grey hues to his hair and beard to great effect. The sheets of paper interlock, so no glue is required for this project.

MATERIALS AND EQUIPMENT

Four A4 sheets of white paper
Coloured felt-tip pens, pencils or paint
Paintbrush (optional)
Pencil
Craft knife
Pair of scissors

METHOD

STEP 1 Transfer the templates onto the paper. Add colour to his face on Fig 7.3a (the first layer, A), page 131, the nose on Figs 7.3b and 7.3c (layers B and C), pages 132–133, and to the eyes, mouth and hat on Fig 7.3d (layer D), page 134. Once complete, paint the reverse side of the hat which folds over at the top.

STEP 2 If you wish, add shading to the bobble and the fur edge of the hat, and to his eyebrows and moustache.

STEP 3 Cut out the four layers making up the face with a craft knife and a pair of scissors, depending on which you find easiest to use, or if you are working with children. Cover the areas already cut with a sheet of white paper to prevent unnecessary creasing.

STEP 4 Using your scissors, snip the eyelashes along the lines on B and C.

STEP 5 Construct the face, starting with A and B. Bring the ends of the moustache together and ease the moustache at B through the slit in layer A and return to its correct alignment.

STEP 6 Gently curl the eyebrows to pass them through the slits in A.

STEP 7 Next take the group of four beards on the chin on B, fold on top of each other to form a layer to slide through the slit in A.

STEP 8 Slot the nose and eyelashes through A; this should be quite easy. Crease the nose and bend the eyelashes into shape.

STEP 9 Carefully slot the hair and beard of B through the corresponding slits in A, starting with the inner slit on the right of the face as you view it. If you find a slot in the layer above that's aligned, pass that piece of hair or beard through it.

STEP 10 Curl the hair by wrapping it around a pencil.

STEP 11 On C, fold the hat brim forwards and crease firmly. Join this layer to the others by first aligning the eyes, then the hair and beard can be passed through the relevant slots in B.

STEP 12 Bend the nose and eyelashes into place.

STEP 13 To add the last layer, position the eyes and mouth, press firmly on the moustache with a finger to hold the layers in place and then slot the hair and beard through the aligned holes. Fold back either side of the brim of Santa's hat and tuck into the slits in D.

STEP 14 Curl the beard, and then fold the hat forward neatly over the curls.

STEP 15 Use the two parallel lines marked on the final template (see Fig 7.3d) to cut and affix your chosen thread or ribbon to the smiling Santa and then you are ready to mount to the wall or a window.

Fig 7.3a

Enlarge all by 132%

Fig 7.3b

Fig 7.3c

Slit

Fig 7.3d

Floral yule log

Here a traditional yule log is decorated with flowers made in paper, thin card or foil (such as that used for pre-packed coffee) which adds a festive note.

MATERIALS AND EQUIPMENT

Brown corrugated card, 241 x 700mm (9½ x 27½in)
Sheet of paper or thin red card, 115 x 152mm (4½ x 6in)
Sheet of paper or thin yellow card, 210 x 70mm (8¼ x 2¾in)
Sheet of paper or thin green card, 172 x 203mm (6¾ x 8in)
Multipurpose adhesive
Seven rubber bands
Metal-edged ruler
Craft knife
Pair of sharp scissors
Needle-nose pliers

METHOD

STEP 1 Begin with the floral yule log itself. Cut the corrugated card into two strips of 700mm (27½in) long: one strip 203mm (8in) wide, and the other 38mm (1½in) wide.

STEP 2 Cut the second, narrower strip in half and tightly roll each 350mm (13¾in) length, ensuring the corrugated side faces outwards. Glue at the ends to secure, holding this in place with rubber bands to dry.

STEP 3 Once dry, remove the bands. Open the wider piece of card, glue the short logs at either end, roll up tightly and secure with glue (and again, use rubber bands to hold in place until dry).

STEP 4 Make the curved flower. Transfer the template (see Fig 7.4a, facing opposite) to the red card and cut out.

STEP 5 Apply a thin line of glue where marked at the ends of petals G and H, then roll them to form two tiny cylinders. These will form stamens.

STEP 6 Pass the ends of petals A, B, C and D down through the central hole, followed by E and F.

STEP 7 Curve these two latter strips around each other and glue together to form a cylinder.

STEP 8 Pass the ends of G and H through the hole, up through the cylinder, and then snip and bend outwards to form the stamens.

STEP 9 Make the cone-shaped flower, starting with a few single petals, to strew over the dining table if you wish. Curl the single strip, taken from the template (see Fig 7.4b), so that point A is aligned with point B. When you are satisfied with the curl, glue together, holding with pliers until set.

STEP 10 Next, form and glue the three petals radiating from the centre of the second template (see Fig 7.4c) and the two petals from the third (see Fig 7.4d), and then glue the two sections together.

STEP 11 Cut the leaves from the green card, cutting a hole in the centre of the leaf for the cone flower to go through.

STEP 12 Glue the leaves and flowers to the log. For the cone flower, cut a small hole in the log to insert the glue and the flower.

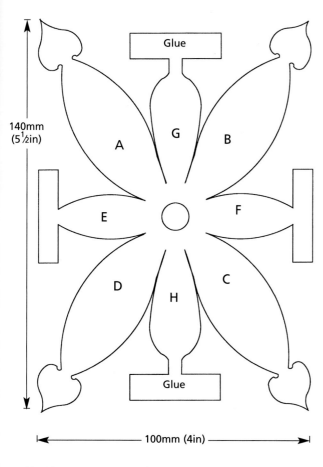

140mm (5½in)

100mm (4in)

Fig 7.4a

Enlarge all by 132%

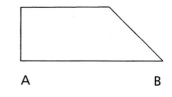

Fig 7.4b

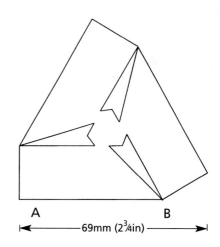

A

69mm (2¾in)

B

Fig 7.4c

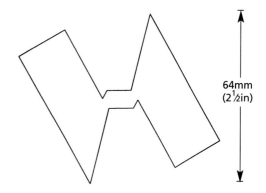

64mm (2½in)

Fig 7.4d

New Year

New Year's Day cards

Celebration gift box

Old year / New year mobile

Chinese lanterns in a vase

New Year's Day cards

These greetings cards make use of sun ray motifs to indicate the dawn of a new year – and there's a clock on the inside, too.

MATERIALS AND EQUIPMENT

A4 sheet of card / Metal-edged ruler / Craft knife

METHOD

STEP 1 Enlarge the template (see Fig 8.1, below), then transfer it onto the card. The black line framing the template indicates the card's dimensions.

STEP 2 Cut out the template, fold the card in four and add your greeting to the inside if you have not completed it on the computer. Execute both variations of the card in the same way.

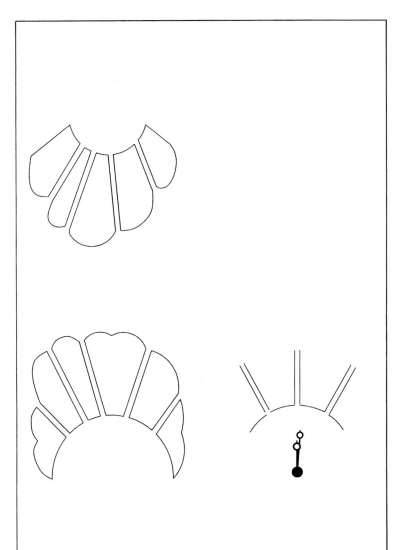

Enlarge by 200%

Fig 8.1

Celebration gift box

This bottle gift bag is the perfect way to present your celebratory bottle of champagne to see the new year in. This design snugly fits a standard wine bottle, but for a larger size, you can alter the dimensions accordingly.

MATERIALS AND EQUIPMENT

Sheet of thick A2 card (desired colour)
Length of ribbon (matching colour)
Coloured pens and/or paints
Metal-edged ruler
Trimming knife
Scoring tool
Multipurpose adhesive
Rubber bands
Two clothes pegs

METHOD

STEP 1 First enlarge the template (see Fig 8.2, overleaf) and then transfer it to a sheet of your chosen card.

STEP 2 Decorate the box and add your greeting or decoration.

STEP 3 Cut out and then score the fold lines.

STEP 4 Roll the card around the bottle.

STEP 5 Cut a strip of card, 19 x 280mm (¾ x 11in).

STEP 6 Apply glue to the base and side tabs and fold around the bottle, gluing as you roll the card. Hold the card in place with several rubber bands and two clothes pegs at the top until dry. Slipping the strip of card on top of the side tab between this and the bands ensures a smooth edge.

STEP 7 To finish, weave a length of ribbon in and out of the cut outs around the top of the gift box, then carefully slide the bottle inside and tie the ribbon in a bow. Cheers!

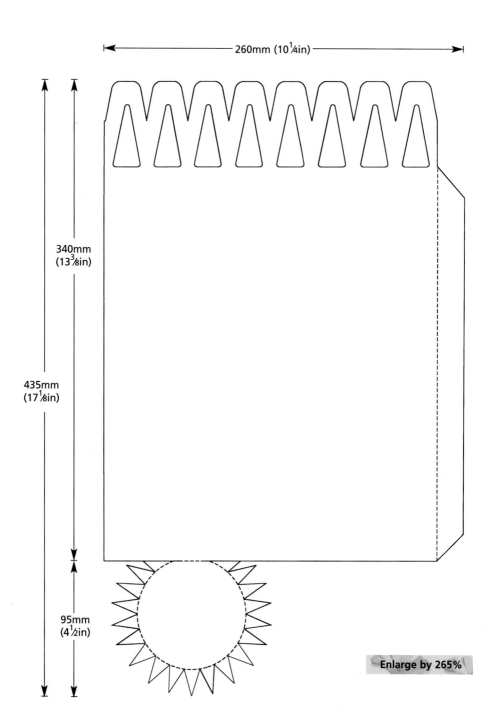

260mm (10¼in)

340mm
(13⅜in)

435mm
(17⅛in)

95mm
(4½in)

Enlarge by 265%

Fig 8.2

Old year/New year mobile

This mobile is based on the well-known image of Janus – the two-faced Roman God who faces both the old and the new year at once. I have adapted the theme to feature Old Father Time on one face instead. If using this mobile as a party decoration, be sure to hang it well out of the way of the New Year revellers.

MATERIALS AND EQUIPMENT

Sheet of thick, yellow card, 305mm (12in) square
Sheet of dark blue card, 280mm (11in) square
Sheet of silver foil-backed card, 280 x 203mm (11 x 8in)
Dinner plate (to use as a template)
Watercolour paints (red, white, yellow and blue)
Gold paint
Multipurpose adhesive
Trimming knife
Pencil
Nylon thread

METHOD

STEP 1 Cut out a circle, 264mm (10⅜in) in diameter, from the sheet of blue card.

STEP 2 Take some foil-backed card – I have used silver, but you can select any contrasting colour – and draw the outlines for some celestial motifs – stars and moons – on one side of the blue card. To the other, add an Old Father Time figure. I have included a white cloud for him to stand on once the shapes are glued in place.

STEP 3 For the reverse side – representing the dawning of the new year – cut the sun from a circle of yellow card, 254mm (10in) in diameter. Mark an inner circle of diameter 203mm (8in) and cut 'flares' around the edge. Cut out the features, paint them and stick them onto the face.

STEP 4 Paint red and gold flares around the edge, glue the face to the blue card and add a length of nylon thread to hang from the ceiling.

Chinese lanterns in a vase

The flowers of the Chinese lantern plant (or bladder cherry) are balloon-like shapes that are surprisingly authentic reproduced in paper. Here, we use the red vase from the sunflower display, but you might also try the gold vase which features the Christmas cacti (see pages 26 and 59) – both are very striking.

MATERIALS AND EQUIPMENT

Sheet of orange gift wrap
Sheet of thick beige or gold card (size dependent on height of stalks)
Watercolour paint (beige)
Multipurpose adhesive
Pencil
Metal-edged ruler
Trimming knife
Paintbrush
Pair of tweezers
Narrow drinking straw

METHOD

STEP 1 Take your sheet of beige or gold card – if you can't find the correct colour, use white card and paint it the appropriate colour. Cut out narrow lengths to form stalks – two or three curved stems leading off the main stem for the individual calyx. If any white card is visible once you have done this, fill in the edges of the stems beige.

STEP 2 Cut a square from the orange wrapping paper. As a guide, the largest lantern is made from a 178mm (7in) square; the smallest from an 89mm (3½in) square. Fold the square in half with the exterior facing outwards, in half again and then diagonally from the point that will be the top centre of the lantern.

STEP 3 Using the template (see Fig 8.3, facing opposite) as a guide, cut the curved section. Open out and make a small hole in the centre, just large enough for the drinking straw to be inserted.

STEP 4 Fold again all the creases into mountain folds.

STEP 5 Next, fold the edge tabs.

STEP 6 Gently curve the sides to form a squared-off top to the lantern.

STEP 7 Glue the tabs, one side at a time, using tweezers to hold together the awkward ones in the smaller lanterns.

STEP 8 Insert the straw in the top hole and blow into it to give it shape. If this is insufficient, form the shape by using the end of the straw to gently work into a lantern.

STEP 9 Take out the straw and glue the lantern onto the beige stalk.

STEP 10 Make further lanterns and glue them to the stems where appropriate – you can make as many as you like.

Actual size

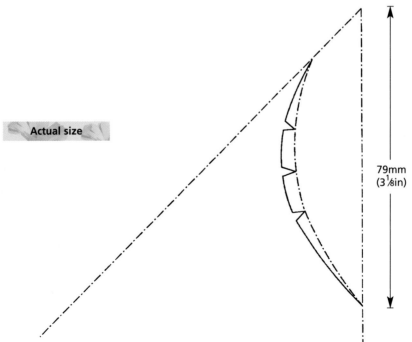

79mm
(3⅛in)

Fig 8.3

About the author

Sìne has always been inspired to make things from paper and card. Raised in a creative household, her parents were passionate about making things: from fashion items to stage costumes, from flannelgraph shapes – remember them? – to models in card and plaster.

Trained as a librarian, Sìne married into an artistic family and, once her children were born, elected to stay at home to raise them. For Sìne, sharing in this all-too-brief period of their childhood has been a privilege and a joy, particularly the fun and creativity experimenting with all kinds of materials – including papercrafts – that they have had together. These experiences are the inspiration for this book.

Index

GMC Publications
BOOKS

TOYMAKING

Scrollsaw Toy Projects	*Ivor Carlyle*
Scrollsaw Toys for All Ages	*Ivor Carlyle*

DOLLS' HOUSES AND MINIATURES

1/12 Scale Character Figures for the Dolls' House	*James Carrington*
Americana in 1/12 Scale: 50 Authentic Projects	
	Joanne Ogreenc & Mary Lou Santovec
Architecture for Dolls' Houses	*Joyce Percival*
The Authentic Georgian Dolls' House	*Brian Long*
A Beginners' Guide to the Dolls' House Hobby	*Jean Nisbett*
Celtic, Medieval and Tudor Wall Hangings in	
1/12 Scale Needlepoint	*Sandra Whitehead*
Creating Decorative Fabrics: Projects in 1/12 Scale	*Janet Storey*
The Dolls' House 1/24 Scale: A Complete Introduction	*Jean Nisbett*
Dolls' House Accessories, Fixtures and Fittings	*Andrea Barham*
Dolls' House Furniture: Easy-to-Make Projects in 1/12 Scale	*Freida Gray*
Dolls' House Makeovers	*Jean Nisbett*
Dolls' House Window Treatments	*Eve Harwood*
Easy to Make Dolls' House Accessories	*Andrea Barham*
Edwardian-Style Hand-Knitted Fashion for 1/12 Scale Dolls	*Yvonne Wakefield*
How to Make Your Dolls' House Special:	
Fresh Ideas for Decorating	*Beryl Armstrong*
Make Your Own Dolls' House Furniture	*Maurice Harper*
Making Dolls' House Furniture	*Patricia King*
Making Georgian Dolls' Houses	*Derek Rowbottom*
Making Miniature Chinese Rugs and Carpets	*Carol Phillipson*
Making Miniature Food and Market Stalls	*Angie Scarr*
Making Miniature Gardens	*Freida Gray*
Making Miniature Oriental Rugs & Carpets	*Meik & Ian McNaughton*
Making Period Dolls' House Accessories	*Andrea Barham*
Making Tudor Dolls' Houses	*Derek Rowbottom*
Making Victorian Dolls' House Furniture	*Patricia King*
Miniature Bobbin Lace	*Roz Snowden*
Miniature Embroidery for the Georgian Dolls' House	*Pamela Warner*
Miniature Embroidery for the Tudor and Stuart Dolls' House	*Pamela Warner*
Miniature Embroidery for the Victorian Dolls' House	*Pamela Warner*
Miniature Needlepoint Carpets	*Janet Granger*
More Miniature Oriental Rugs & Carpets	*Meik & Ian McNaughton*
Needlepoint 1/12 Scale: Design Collections for the Dolls' House	*Felicity Price*
New Ideas for Miniature Bobbin Lace	*Roz Snowden*
The Secrets of the Dolls' House Makers	*Jean Nisbett*

CRAFTS

American Patchwork Designs in Needlepoint	*Melanie Tacon*
A Beginners' Guide to Rubber Stamping	*Brenda Hunt*
Beginning Picture Marquetry	*Lawrence Threadgold*
Blackwork: A New Approach	*Brenda Day*
Celtic Cross Stitch Designs	*Carol Phillipson*
Celtic Knotwork Designs	*Sheila Sturrock*
Celtic Knotwork Handbook	*Sheila Sturrock*
Celtic Spirals and Other Designs	*Sheila Sturrock*
Complete Pyrography	*Stephen Poole*
Creative Backstitch	*Helen Hall*
Creative Embroidery Techniques Using Colour Through Gold	
	Daphne J. Ashby & Jackie Woolsey
The Creative Quilter: Techniques and Projects	*Pauline Brown*
Cross-Stitch Designs from China	*Carol Phillipson*
Decoration on Fabric: A Sourcebook of Ideas	*Pauline Brown*
Decorative Beaded Purses	*Enid Taylor*
Designing and Making Cards	*Glennis Gilruth*
Glass Engraving Pattern Book	*John Everett*
Glass Painting	*Emma Sedman*
Handcrafted Rugs	*Sandra Hardy*
How to Arrange Flowers: A Japanese Approach to English Design	*Taeko Marvelly*
How to Make First-Class Cards	*Debbie Brown*
An Introduction to Crewel Embroidery	*Mave Glenny*

Making and Using Working Drawings for	
Realistic Model Animals	*Basil F. Fordham*
Making Character Bears	*Valerie Tyler*
Making Decorative Screens	*Amanda Howes*
Making Fabergé-Style Eggs	*Denise Hopper*
Making Fairies and Fantastical Creatures	*Julie Sharp*
Making Greetings Cards for Beginners	*Pat Sutherland*
Making Hand-Sewn Boxes: Techniques and Projects	*Jackie Woolsey*
Making Knitwear Fit	*Pat Ashforth & Steve Plummer*
Making Mini Cards, Gift Tags & Invitations	*Glennis Gilruth*
Making Soft-Bodied Dough Characters	*Patricia Hughes*
Natural Ideas for Christmas: Fantastic Decorations to Make	
	Josie Cameron-Ashcroft & Carol Cox
New Ideas for Crochet: Stylish Projects for the Home	*Darsha Capaldi*
Papercraft Projects for Special Occasions	*Sine Chesterman*
Patchwork for Beginners	*Pauline Brown*
Pyrography Designs	*Norma Gregory*
Pyrography Handbook (Practical Crafts)	*Stephen Poole*
Rose Windows for Quilters	*Angela Besley*
Rubber Stamping with Other Crafts	*Lynne Garner*
Sponge Painting	*Ann Rooney*
Stained Glass: Techniques and Projects	*Mary Shanahan*
Step-by-Step Pyrography Projects for the Solid Point Machine	*Norma Gregory*
Tassel Making for Beginners	*Enid Taylor*
Tatting Collage	*Lindsay Rogers*
Tatting Patterns	*Lyn Morton*
Temari: A Traditional Japanese Embroidery Technique	*Margaret Ludlow*
Trip Around the World: 25 Patchwork, Quilting and	
Appliqué Projects	*Gail Lawther*
Trompe l'Oeil: Techniques and Projects	*Jan Lee Johnson*
Tudor Treasures to Embroider	*Pamela Warner*
Wax Art	*Hazel Marsh*

MAGAZINES

WOODTURNING ✦ WOODCARVING

FURNITURE & CABINETMAKING

THE ROUTER ✦ WOODWORKING

THE DOLLS' HOUSE MAGAZINE

OUTDOOR PHOTOGRAPHY ✦ BLACK & WHITE

PHOTOGRAPHY ✦ MACHINE KNITTING NEWS

BUSINESSMATTERS

The above represents a full list of all titles currently published or
scheduled to be published.

All are available direct from the Publishers or through bookshops,
newsagents and specialist retailers.

To place an order, or to obtain a complete catalogue, contact:

GMC Publications,
Castle Place, 166 High Street, Lewes, East Sussex
BN7 1XU, United Kingdom
Tel: 01273 488005 Fax: 01273 478606
E-mail: pubs@thegmcgroup.com

Orders by credit card are accepted